CURTAIN UP!

Greg King

Steven Stead

Charon Williams-Ros

Tina Le Roux

Janine
Bennewith-
Van Wyk

Peter Court

Illa Thompson

Shelley McLean

CURTAIN UP!

How to Stage
Great Youth Productions

Edited by Charon Williams-Ros

Illustrated by Greg King

NICK HERN BOOKS
London
www.nickhernbooks.co.uk

A Nick Hern Book

Curtain Up!
first published in Great Britain in 2023
by Nick Hern Books Limited,
The Glasshouse, 49a Goldhawk Road,
London W12 8QP

Designed and typeset by Nick Hern Books
Printed and bound in Great Britain by 4Edge Limited, Essex

A CIP catalogue record for this book is available
from the British Library

ISBN 978 1 84842 852 2

CONTENTS

INTRODUCTION

Curtain Up! serves as a highly accessible, introductory guide to theatre-making for any school, college, amateur or semi-professional theatre company. Each member of our team has experienced the frustration of not having enough time to assist more than a handful of the drama teachers or youth theatre groups who have asked for help with their productions. This is our solution: a comprehensive guide which contains the relevant information we believe will take any production to the next level.

Like theatre, this book is a collaborative effort where each member of a professional production team reveals the essence of their specific craft. As it is written by a team, it should be read by a team, either in its entirety or by those chapters relevant to their job descriptions.

You can find a useful resources pack to download, print and share at www.nickhernbooks/curtain-up

We hope you find *Curtain Up!* useful, and wish you all the very best with your productions!

Charon Williams-Ros

Chapter One

DIRECTION

Steven Stead

Steven Stead is a multi-award-winning actor and director who has directed opera, drama, pantomime, comedy and musical theatre. He is the executive director of Kickstart Productions.

Directing professional adult actors, amateur actors, or casts of young actors is fundamentally the same job: You have to be one-third team leader, one-third psychiatrist, and one-third nursery-school teacher! And the basic tenet of being a director is the same for whoever you are directing:

*You are there to make sure that the story
the actors are there to tell is being well told.*

Every piece of information that an audience receives in the process of watching a story told by actors – whether that information is visual, aural, or emotionally subliminal – is important. The actors cannot ever fully appreciate the impact that their movements, their positions, the underscoring music, the scenery, the costumes or the lighting might be having on an audience, because they are *in* the picture. But the director sits outside the picture, as an audience member might, and acts as an editor and facilitator, and guinea pig, constantly checking the semiotics being transmitted from the stage – *which is just a posh way of saying checking the flow of communication from the stage to the audience.*

How a director goes about this very specific and sometimes very lonely job is very subjective, and varies widely from director to director. But every director has a *process*, no matter how much it may differ from their colleagues. And that process will include certain common fundamentals covering preparation, casting, scheduling and staging. Though there might be vastly divergent opinions on the more esoteric aspects of theatre-making, like textual analysis, voice work, workshopping and movement exploration, these four practical elements should be part of any director's process, whether they are doing *Red Riding Hood* at a kindergarten or *King Lear* at the Royal Shakespeare Company.

Before we take a look at the practical aspects of putting a production together, it is worth saying that when working with young people especially, one should have a much stronger sense of structure and intention than one might need with experienced adults. There is no doubt that children have enormous amounts of creative energy and often vivid imaginations, but in order for these to truly be unleashed and harnessed, they need structure and order, and a clear sense of common purpose.

PREPARATION

This part of the director's journey is hugely personal and very private. It would begin with choosing the material. Or, very often, being told by your headteacher to *'Do something for the Year 5's next term',* ...and then having the headache of choosing the material.

When you are looking for a play or a musical, or a story that you are hoping to workshop a production around, be realistic about the time you have, and the talent at your disposal. If you only have a short rehearsal period (and for young people anything less than four weeks is short), you are better off doing a short one-act play, perhaps with a few simple songs and a small cast. Don't choose a book musical like Disney's *Beauty and the Beast* because those big shows need much more rehearsal time because of the music and choreography that has to be learned.

> *In my experience, every minute of stage time in a musical number requires an hour and a half of dedicated rehearsal time just to get blocked or sketched out, let alone polished.*

Similarly, if you know that you have a couple of really good actors, who are not the strongest singers, don't choose a musical like *West Side Story* just because you love it! There is no shame in choosing something modest in scale and doing it well.

When you are looking for a show and your local library only has *The Complete Works of Shakespeare* and a couple of murder mysteries from the 1940s, don't despair. The internet is a wonderful tool, and you can find almost anything you could wish for. Search online for 'Plays with 15 Characters' and check out the great websites that come up which are sure to inspire you. Sites like applays.com, Concord Theatricals and Nick Hern Books will be full of inspiring scripts at reasonable prices.

Whether you decide to write your own piece or use one already written, analyse it carefully:

○ *How many scenes are there?*

○ *What scenic/visual elements do those scenes require?*

Divide the piece up into manageable chunks to make creating a rehearsal schedule easier:

- *How many actors are required?*
- *Can I fit in additional cast somewhere if I need to bump up cast numbers?*
- *VERY IMPORTANTLY: What is this play/musical about? Does it have a message or a central theme? And how does it make me feel?*

That last point is very important because it is your point of creative departure, and it is this little nugget of understanding or feeling that you will be communicating to your cast, which will serve as a foundation and as a goal as the process continues. Even when you are in a slough of despair and feel that it'll never come right (and don't worry, everyone feels like this at some point), hang onto that essence of what makes the piece resonate with you personally, because then you can steer the ship in the right direction. Without having a clear understanding and relationship with the piece, you will flounder, make random choices, and be a poor leader. If you don't feel something for the piece, or don't really understand it, don't do it. Even if you are doing a simple kids' play and your principal feeling is a sense that it is just a joyous romp, hang onto that doggedly.

And when it stops being a joyous romp, start working at making it one, or fix the bits that are stopping it from being a joyous romp!

COPYRIGHT

It is very important that you realise that all published material is subject to copyright and may not be performed without a licence to do so. This includes all performances where there is going to be any sort of an audience, whether they are a paying audience or not. The only exception may be if you are doing an extract of a play or book as a part of a lesson in a classroom or a private reading. But the moment you have any spectators at all, you do need to obtain permission from the rights-holders. Some material falls into the 'public domain', usually writers who have died seventy years or more prior to the intended performance. This makes works by writers like Shakespeare, Christopher Marlowe or Oscar Wilde, for example, copyright-free.

However, if you choose an ancient Greek play or similar, thinking that it must be out of copyright by virtue of it being in the public domain for over two thousand years, the translation or edition you are using will, in all likelihood, have been written and published relatively recently and will need to be licensed. You can find out who the rights-holders are and where to contact them for permission to perform, on the first page of most published plays or scores. It is also worth noting that there is a different licence, pricing structure and often even a different licensor depending on whether you are applying for amateur or professional rights. So, know which you require. (If you are not paying your actors, or they are students, then you are looking to secure an amateur licence.)

A heads-up about musical scores: although many operas and operettas are out of copyright, their orchestral parts are not and need to be bought or rented from the publishers of the musical scores.

CONCEPT

Another vital area of preparation is choosing your concept.

This is essentially deciding how you are going to present the piece you have chosen. It is a really creative and potentially fun and rewarding part of the process, because there are no wrong answers, and there is no one sitting in judgement over you. Let your imagination run wild! *But keep reminding it of practicalities like budget and time!*

You can conceptualise on your own or in collaboration with a design team if you have such a luxury. Chatting freely with your set and/or costume designer can often unlock your concept more fully and push you out of your immediate comfort zones.

Your concept might be as simple as choosing a period or colour theme.

For example, you might elect to do *The Pied Piper* set in the Middle Ages, with costume and scenery themes in the jewel colours and style of stained glass of the period. Or you could decide to set the same play on a Caribbean island in the nineteenth century and use a colour theme of red, yellow and green, the Reggae colours. Do you see? The same play, but vastly different concepts.

The theatre offers hugely diverse possibilities in terms of concepts for shows. There are no rules. Well... no rules except:

Actors must be audible and visible.

But whether you decide to set *Treasure Island* around a swimming pool, or do a promenade performance of *Dracula* where the cast lead the audience from spooky basements to echoing courtyard, always ensure that the spaces you've chosen can be adequately lit and amplified if necessary. Very often your concept will germinate from that little nugget of affinity or understanding that you have identified in the early part of preparation, because that is your own creative imagination leading your choices.

There is, however, absolutely nothing wrong with just staging a production the good old-fashioned way on a proscenium arch stage and opening and closing the curtain when you want to do a scene change.

Although you might have reservations about this approach not being innovative enough, it's worked for centuries so why knock it now? As long as what is revealed when that curtain rises has been fully conceptualised, or thought through from moment to moment, and helps to tell the audience the story.

Remember, making theatre is fundamentally all about the storytelling.

Your concept may be very visually oriented, and so, if you are not a dab hand with a paint brush or hammer and nails, it is good to have someone who understands your concept and can help you realise it. You might be influenced in your vision for sets and costumes by a myriad of stimuli ranging from:

○ *Classical Greek sculpture to Disney cartoons.*

○ *The abstract squares of Mondrian and Rothko to the super-realistic works of Rembrandt, Edward Hopper or Norman Rockwell.*

○ *Travel writing, your own travels, or a friend's holiday snaps of the Amazon or the Sahara.*

The sources of inspiration for creating a concept are plentiful. Explore them! And get your designers to come on the journey with you, adding their own details and touches to flesh out and fulfil your vision.

CASTING

I have heard it said by other directors that 80% of a director's job is casting. Cast it well and the show does itself. Well... I agree to some extent. The right personalities can certainly make a production come alive in a spectacular way. But a director still needs to steer even the most experienced actor in the right direction.

In an educational environment, there will always be a couple of kids who you know have the goods to play certain roles. They are the charismatic or obviously talented individuals who you can't help but notice. Cast them by all means. They will be the backbone of your cast. But there will also be many shy or introverted kids just waiting for an opportunity to express themselves who could really surprise you. It's worth taking a chance on them. Hold auditions, give everyone a chance to shine, and then follow your instincts. They will invariably be right.

In auditioning your cast, make sure that they prepare something for you, a poem, a speech, or a song if appropriate, and hear them one by one. Don't let them read cold from the script. Very few experienced professionals are good sight-readers (and children usually are not!). Sometimes, a good way of auditioning is to hold a group movement session. For example, if you have decided to produce *Pinnochio,* describe each character and get everyone to create their own little scene or improvised movement: Pinocchio, Geppetto, Blue Fairy, Fox and Cat... you'll soon see which performers have affinities with which energies and who shows the most potential in each role. Again, the results could surprise you!

Quite often, if you take a risk casting someone unlikely, you can be very pleasantly surprised at how they grow with the challenge. But equally, don't put these types in key positions in the cast. If they should experience a loss of confidence for any reason, or prove unequal to the task, it's not a train crash if they are playing a small role, but it's a problem for you, and for them, if they're playing the lead!

SCHEDULING

I know this sounds boring, but honestly it is a major part of being a director. By scheduling carefully you are not only managing your production's development to opening night, you are managing your cast's expectations in terms of their time and commitment, and this is hugely important. I know directors who keep their entire cast hanging around for hours in the rehearsal room even when there is only a scene for two or three characters being rehearsed. This (especially with young people) creates an atmosphere of boredom and frustration which is hugely counterproductive to the creative process. Engaged, active minds and bodies are more receptive and productive.

Here is an example of what a schedule might look like.

Mon 1 April	2.30pm:	Cinderella, Buttons (Scene 1)
	3.00pm:	+Fairy Godmother
	3.30pm:	+Ugly Sisters, Prince
		(for big song end Scene 1)
	(5pm finish)	
Tues 2 April	2.30pm:	Cinderella, Buttons, Fairy Godmother, Ugly Sisters and Prince (Recap Scene 1)
	(4pm finish)	
	4pm:	Forest Creatures (Ballet)
	(5pm finish)	

Do you see why breaking the piece down into chunks is a necessary idea?

- *Allow about half an hour for every three pages of text, and at least an hour for any musical rehearsal.*
- *Schedule breaks! You need them and so do the cast. Every hour and a half, take ten minutes.*
- *Stick to your schedule wherever possible. It gives you and your cast a sense of structure, support, and is a constant reminder of your ultimate goal.*

If you run out of time and don't finish the scene you scheduled, don't work late to complete the work. It's not fair on you or the cast. Of course, five minutes' overtime won't harm anyone, but working way over the scheduled cut-off time sends all the wrong messages:

- *That the schedule is flexible and irrelevant, so arriving late is not a big deal.*
- *That you as a leader do not have a handle on the work you are doing.*

It creates a sense of instability and a luck of trust. It's better to finish when you said you would, and go home and find a spot in your future schedule to make an adjustment to accommodate that scene. No one minds small changes if they are given a bit of warning. Build an hour's vague 'recap' time into a weekly schedule which you can use to catch up if you are behind for any reason. You can detail these on the schedule with:

    Fri 5 April   2.30pm: Recap: Cast TBD (to be detailed)

Then the cast know that they might be called for that rehearsal and will wait on you to tell them.

REHEARSALS

I have touched on aspects of staging in the section on Concept, where you can choose what context or space you want to stage your production in the grand scale. So I would like to explore the intimate elements of staging a production: working with the actors in the rehearsal studio.

Okay. You have a script. You have a cast. It's your first rehearsal. What do you do?

Blocking: This is literally the opposite of what it sounds like! To block actually means to free the play up physically and choose the movements the actors will make.

Well, before you block, a full cast read-through is a really good idea. Get the whole company and all your technical team in from the word go, and involved from the very first step. This is a good time to chat briefly to them about your concept, about the journey you are all embarking on, and to show them some of the designs or reference material that have inspired you. This will in turn inspire them, and give them a sense of focus and ownership.

Read-throughs can be dreadful, so don't despair! Actors overact or underact out of insecurity, and often misread lines, stressing all the wrong words. Just smile and make a mental note to fix those things in rehearsal.

A read-through is just about putting your collective toes in the water before the big plunge!

So, your read-through was a moderate success, and you have your first blocking rehearsal: a crowd scene in a marketplace involving fifteen actors. Where to start?

It is generally regarded as a fact that all acting is about motivation. And that the best acting is actually about reacting. Your blocking is going to come out of these forces, which will shape your and the actors' choices, and which can often be very organic.

Give every actor a name and a character, even if they are just in the chorus.

Give them a bit of a backstory:

◉ *They have a sore leg and are trying to beg for money to see a doctor.*

- *They are shopping for quality trout because Aunty's coming for dinner.*

- *They are looking for a lost dog.*

- *They are late for (or waiting for) a romantic assignation.*

Then give them various entrance points dotted around the set, through doors or archways you may have in mind. You can mark these up on the floor with tape, or use chairs to mark them and keep the acting space consistent and proportional.

Use levels if you can. It's more interesting to see people moving through space on different levels than just flat across the floor level. Then give them points they should aim for, or a vague pattern to achieve over the course of the scene.

Don't let them stand in lines! Dot them around in groups of twos and threes. Fill the stage with bodies in interesting angles and positions.

And then let them improvise. If they are clear about what their motivation is:

- *The need for a doctor.*

- *The fear of the awful aunty.*

- *The panic of looking for a lost dog.*

- *The anticipation of romance.*

You suddenly have a dynamic crowd scene full of texture and movement. Of course, you can shape this, tweak it, invent certain interactions, alter some patterns or levels of play, but you have a stage full of actors who are clear about what their motivation is, and who are reacting to one another.

Remember, it is not what each actor is saying or doing themselves, but their impact on those they are interacting with that creates drama.

This is an important element to appreciate when you are blocking a scene. It will dictate or direct almost every move. Moves and gestures must be motivated by something and they will have an effect on everyone else on that stage.

If you can keep up the inner emotional logic of the movements so that nothing jars and everything makes sense and has consequence, then your blocking will have a fluidity and natural quality which most non-theatre-makers would take completely for granted as just having happened organically. They will have no idea of the sweat and detail that went into forging every moment! If not, the work will flicker and stick like an early black-and-white silent movie, making the audience uncomfortable and disengaged.

Don't be afraid to allow the actors to choose their own movements, but every time they make a choice, ask them why they are doing it. If they can't answer, don't let them do it.

Or suggest another possibility that might make more logical sense.

You: Joanne, why did you cross the stage when you said 'Well, I wouldn't know about that'?

Joanne: I don't know. It just felt right.

You: It could work, but it looks a bit contrived. Maybe your character is going to get a pot from the cupboard over there to start her cooking. And she's fed up with the chap she's talking to, so she's doing it in a grumpy way. But she doesn't want him to know that she's grumpy because he is her boss. Try it again.

And watch it come to life.

Get your actors to listen to each other. Nothing is more deathly than a bunch of actors just waiting for a chance to say their lines. They must speak as a result of what they have heard.

CHARACTERISATION

Obviously, acting involves playing characters that are often very different from the actor's own attributes. You may choose (or be forced) to cast someone young to play an old person, or a thin person to play a fat one, or a slight person to play a muscular brute. This poses challenges to you as a director, and to your actors. With your help and guidance, they have to transform their bodies and voices to suit the roles that they have been cast in.

THE BODY

It ultimately all comes down to *energy*: Where are the energy centres in the body of the actor, and where do they have to shift to in order to play the character?

This may sound a bit esoteric, but it is actually very practical. There have been many revelatory studies of movement for dancers that are applicable to actors, such as Rudolf von Laban's analysis of the body's effort actions, that are well worth dipping into. But, you can begin addressing the situation yourself.

Everybody holds tension in different places, giving a different distribution of energy centres in the body. Some people have high energy centres, with braced chests, and lead with the chest or the head when they walk; others lead with their pelvis; some have low energy centres pulling them towards the ground and making them slower movers, or their weight lists from side to side when they walk.

Asking actors to look in a mirror and begin to attempt to identify where their own energy centres and areas of tension are is the first step towards body-awareness.

The next step is to analyse their own walk and note how energy and tension shifts around the body when it moves. A good way to do this is to split your actors into pairs, and have each one watch the other walking across a room. Then get the observer to mimic the walk in a way that exaggerates the mannerisms or characteristics of their partner. You need to manage this by pointing out the accurate observations and refining any gross exaggerations. The other way to do this is to have one actor walk in front and the other to follow behind, gradually taking on the attributes of the person in front.

Another wonderful movement game is to play with the notion of pelvic placement. Get the actors to imagine that they have a shallow basin of water lying on top of their pelvis, then tip the basin forward slightly, and walk across the room trying not to 'spill' any. Repeat the exercise, this time tilting the basin backwards. The 'walks' will change radically, and this can be very helpful to explore other different ways of carrying energy in the body. It can be used to find a different movement vocabulary for playing an older person, a larger person, a self-consciously sexy, or shy person.

Ask the actors to explore what happens when they shift their energy centres to other parts of their bodies when walking. Also, holding the weight high up in the upper body, as opposed to dropping the energy to the pelvic floor, creates diametrically opposite characters: the high energy centre being either full of self-importance or arrogance, or even aggression or defensiveness; and the low energy centre being more passive, with a less confrontational relationship with the world befitting gentler, low-status characters.

Finding a neutral stance where the spine is aligned, the feet parallel and the pelvis perfectly level is a very helpful point of departure. You can then give suggestions, or instructions such as:

> 'This old lady is very sad. Allow your shoulders and neck to give in to gravity. Feel your energy centre shift from your chest to your lower belly.'

Then, let them walk with this new energy. You, and they, will be amazed at the rapid physical insights you can achieve in this manner. It can be a very releasing exercise and help shift the actor away from their own physical comfort zones.

Of course, you can also add animal suggestions for character: ask them to add a bird's energy to their character, explore a dabbing, nervous, rapid energy. Or a cat's – to explore a sensual, flowing energy. Or a rhino to feel the heavy push and solid, earthbound flow of energy. The possibilities are actually endless. Pick an animal that you think embodies the character and get the actor to, firstly, explore being that animal. Then, gradually work up to being a person with the attributes of that animal.

THE VOICE

In the same way as the body needs to be transformed, the voice, too, often needs to be altered. A good way to begin most vocal work is to 'siren', to move without pressure on the voice, from the lowest natural notes in the voice to the highest in the head-voice. Up and down, easy and effortless, allowing the actor to feel the full range at their disposal, with many more tones than they would ever use in their 'normal' voice. This exercise can actually develop range at both ends of the voice if done regularly and without stress or straining.

Choose a simple sentence or nursery rhyme and try it out using different tones: place it in the nasal resonators as if you have a cold. Say it fast. Then, say it very slowly. Place the voice in different parts of the body, and imagine it resonating in the jaw, the forehead, the chest, the back. Explore speed of speech in each area. Obviously, not all of these will be the right approach for all characters, but it is a way of finding a voice for your character.

Exploring other accents is also helpful in transforming into other characters, as each accent places the voice in different parts of the body, and usually has its own idiosyncrasies in terms of speed, cadence and tone.

Basically, get your actors to explore what it feels like to be other than what they feel they are. And give them practical ways of being able to slip into this other skin, by using a consciousness of energy, tension and speed to change their own body patterns to those of their character.

PRODUCTION WEEK

As the performance dates get closer, you will need to schedule the technical week, i.e. your set-up on stage, your lighting and sound rehearsal, and your dress rehearsals. This is very important and requires liaison with your designers and technicians in these departments.

Make sure your design team and technicians have enough time to do what they need to do, but that they work within a larger framework which allows time for everything that needs to happen.

The technical week and dress rehearsals are fraught in any production. You, as a director (and therefore the final word in any production), can make it much smoother and more bearable by creating a solid technical schedule. It is advisable to do this in conjunction with your stage manager, if you are lucky enough to have one.

I strongly advise getting someone to stage manage your production, whether it is a strong-minded staff/ committee member or a sensible, competent student. They will be your eyes, ears and hands backstage when you can no longer be there.

In order to plan a technical schedule, you need to remember that, while lighting, set and sound teams can work simultaneously with one another, they all actually need some dedicated time on their own. Lighting always needs to come first, because they need a near-empty stage to rig (hanging lights in the correct positions), and attach gels (the filters in front of lights which give them their colour).

By this time the set should be built, because the lighting department cannot do the next part of their job, which is to focus (pointing the lights in the right direction), making sure the areas of the set you need lit in certain ways are lit.

The lighting designer then needs to plot with the director. This is a long and potentially tedious experience that can be stressful when there are time constraints, but it is a very important part of any production. These sessions can be led by the director if you have a very clear idea about what you want (and it is certainly quicker if you do), or by the lighting designer, but a collaboration between both is ideal. The sound team may use this time to set up monitors, cabling, microphones and any other equipment they, or you, may feel is necessary.

While the lights are being plotted, the set designer and their team can continue dressing the set, but they will of course have to do it by torchlight, because they will constantly be plunged into darkness. For safety's sake, someone must yell out *'Going to black!'* before you do.

Once the set is up and the lighting is rigged and plotted, you are ready for the sound department. If you are doing a musical with individual radio microphones, sound will need to be left alone in the auditorium to make a lot of noise on their own. This is the best time to sneak off and have dinner or a long coffee!

Once this is done, you will be ready for the cast. Don't let them near the theatre until this point. They will only get in the way and drive you and your technical team mad. Start them with a *placing call*, a rehearsal literally moving through the whole show, placing them in the correct positions on the stage/set.

Your next rehearsal will be a technical one, working through the piece with lights and sound. Costumes can be added now, if you are brave or are short of time. Before your first rehearsal with sound, you will need to schedule a sound check, which should take a couple of hours.

Then dress rehearsals with full technical until your FDR (Final Dress Rehearsal) which is the last rehearsal you will have before an audience sees your work.

Of course, every show and every theatre or institution will bring its own constraints or requirements, but whatever the dictates of your cast and theatre availability or staging requirements, make sure that you have allocated time for all the elements to come together in that order. You will be avoiding a bun fight and several nervous breakdowns.

During all the dress and technical rehearsals, directors should be in the auditorium seeing everything from the front as the audience does, and writing notes about what is wrong and what needs fixing/changing. *Don't* be tempted to help put on wigs backstage or sort out the broken smoke machine. Get stage management to do all this. It is not your job. The director's job is to direct all these various elements and weld them into a cohesive whole.

FINAL WORD

Whatever your concept, whatever your cast's level of experience or ability, always be honest about your choices. Know why you are making them and make them boldly and with relish. If you work from a place of confidence and delight in the work, then your cast will follow you to the moon and back.

RESOURCES

STAGE DIRECTIONS

Backstage: That part of the stage that is out of view of the audience.

Blocking: The director's process of arranging the actors' movements in each scene. These are recorded in the script by the stage manager or assistant stage manager.

Downstage: The area of the stage closest to the audience.

House: The auditorium.

Placing call: The first cast rehearsal in the theatre where the production team 'places' the cast in specific positions on set for each scene.

Playing area: The performance space within which the actor is in full view of the audience.

Upstage: Towards the back wall of the stage.

USL: Upstage left.

USR: Upstage right.

Stage left/Prompt: The actor's left when they're facing the audience.

Stage right/OP (Opposite Prompt): The actor's right when they're facing the audience.

Wings: The out-of-view area on each side of the stage.

TIPS FOR ACTORS AUDITIONING

What am I going to perform?

You're going to need to select an appropriate piece for an acting audition, but don't panic. Narrow down your selection:

Style: If you're auditioning for Shakespeare, don't select a piece from *Winnie the Pooh*.

Range: The piece must contain enough emotional range to show what you can do.

Length: It doesn't have to be long – just impactful.

It should also be age appropriate.

How am I going to remember the lines?

Don't just sit and try and learn them! There's a process:

Make sense of them first. Do you understand what the character is going through? Does every line make absolute sense to you?

Break the piece up into smaller chunks and map out the emotional journey – e.g. In the first few lines she suspects something is wrong. In the next three lines she realises that her friend has betrayed her. In the next four lines she breaks down, and in the last few lines she gets angry and plots her revenge.

Find the **key words** in each section. These are the foundations you'll build on.

How am I going to perform it?

Put your character into a setting – e.g. Where was she when she began to suspect something? The kitchen? What was she doing? Baking? Well, now you can introduce a prop to work with. A prop can turn a monologue on its head. A serious monologue can become funny if the character is holding an inappropriate or surprising prop throughout the entire thing – e.g. a cake. Plot out some movements for your character that seem to come naturally. Maybe she's about to throw the cake, decides against it, and eats it instead.

How will I know if my performance is any good?

Perform it for someone you respect before the audition. A drama teacher is an obvious choice. Be open to constructive criticism.

How do I overcome my nerves on the day?

It's normal to be nervous for auditions. Let your nerves feed your performance. Other ways you can prepare are:

- *Do a physical warm-up. You are less likely to freeze if your muscles are warm. Don't forget your jaw, tongue and lips.*
- *Do a vocal warm-up. Your voice needs to be relaxed.*
- *Run through your piece beforehand.*

Get out of the audience and into your own body! You can't try and assess yourself from the outside.

Now go to the mirror, look at yourself and say, 'You're amazing!' Now you're ready for your acting audition.

THE ELEMENTS OF COMPOSITION

Composition means the arrangement of visual elements. This is particularly helpful in directing group scenes.

Unity: Do all the elements (characters in relation to the set and props) look as though they belong together or does something look awkward or out of place? Remember all the characters in each scene should be contributing to the same story.

Balance: A symmetrical composition adds a sense of calm, whereas an asymmetrical composition will create imbalance and unease.

Movement: It does not have to be a high-energy scene to create visual movement. A character's eyes following an imaginary moving object can sometimes suffice.

Rhythm: Repetition of shapes, colour or movement can create a pleasing rhythm. (Consider the costumes your cast are wearing when you create these pictures.)

Focus: A focal point is necessary, otherwise the viewer's eye wanders around not knowing where they should be looking.

Contrast: Strong differences between light and dark help to highlight certain areas and characters. This can be established with costume, lighting or characterisation.

Pattern: Be aware of the lines and patterns in your compositions.

Proportion: How big, small, near and distant all fit together.

Chapter Two

VOCAL DIRECTION

Shelley McLean

Shelley McLean is an award-winning singer and vocal director who is much in demand as a voice coach. She divides her time between teaching, performing and musical direction.

The voice is the actor/singer's instrument. A vital tool that can enhance or transform a character. It is also flexible and, most exciting of all, trainable!

Basic vocal exercises for range and flexibility work equally well for both actors and singers, bringing life to the words they speak and the lyrics they sing.

This chapter deals primarily with the direction of vocals in a musical, but the basic principles apply for all performance involving the voice.

PREPARATION

Effective preparation will give you confidence, and will make it possible for you to begin the rehearsals with both a vision and a plan of how to get there. So, get cracking!

Before you have even met, both you and the performers are already working towards a common goal: a successful audition. With that in mind, make sure the information you provide beforehand leaves them in no doubt as to what you are looking for.

AUDITION PREP FOR THE SINGER

When sending out information regarding the singing audition, be clear about what you want to hear. It's a good idea to give examples of musical styles/genres that will assist hopeful performers with their preparation.

Should there be an audition pianist available, perhaps include their e-mail address in your audition notice – but only if the pianist is happy with this. This will make it possible for the pianist to see the music before the audition.

It is the performer's responsibility to ensure that the written key is suitable for them, and they need to confirm this.

If you are allowing them to audition using backing tracks, make sure they know to bring in two copies of the track in whichever format they have chosen in case of malfunction. Also, let them know which technologies you can support – e.g. CD, memory stick, iPod.

AUDITION PREP FOR YOU

It is vital that you have a very clear idea of what you are looking for in terms of vocal range and performance before you even begin the audition process:

O *Make sure you are extremely familiar with the show material and what the various roles require.*

O *Be very clear about what notes need to be hit and in which song.*

O *Make sure there is a piano/keyboard for the accompanist if necessary, and/or a CD player/iPod station/laptop with speakers for backing tracks.*

O *It is essential to have a clear idea of what the director's casting priorities are. You may audition someone who fits the singing role to perfection, but isn't quite what the director is looking for, in terms of acting and dancing skills.*

It is important to remember that the correct vocal fit is vital not just for the character's solo parts but for the group numbers as well. The soloist's ability to harmonise and their contribution to the overall vocal blend affects the musical quality of the entire show.

THE AUDITION

Confidence is key: Set the tone for the audition room. Very few people perform well in a tense atmosphere. The more relaxed the singers are, the better they will perform.

ICE-BREAKERS

You have the power to make the audition fun and exciting, but also as relaxed as possible. Here are some ways to set a relaxed tone for the entire audition, so you are more likely to see what the performers can do:

O *Welcome everyone into the audition space.*

O *In a friendly manner, explain the day's proceedings.*

- *Do a quick five-minute vocal warm-up. Include simple but effective exercises like five-note scales throughout the ranges, arpeggios and perhaps some octaves.*

- *Play a vocal game – e.g. use a little ditty which is catchy, quick-to-learn and that the auditionees can all sing together. Once they know it, you can use it as a fun ice-breaker.*

Distraction is a great technique especially with young people who can work themselves (and their peers) into a nervous frenzy. The following yogic breathing technique will help to relax and focus them:

- *Block your left nostril with one finger and take a deep breath in through the right nostril.*

- *Now block your right nostril and breathe out of the left... and in again through the left.*

- *Block your left nostril and breathe out of your right nostril... and in again through the right.*

- *Swap and repeat.*

This exercise facilitates diaphragmatic breathing without the auditionees being aware of it.

WHAT YOU ARE LOOKING FOR

Whether you are auditioning young people or adults, it is important to have a realistic grasp of their basic abilities.

The type of production your director has chosen will determine your needs to a degree, but there are some hard-and-fast rules that apply to all auditions.

You are looking for:

- *Clarity of sound, not a sound that's being squashed through the nose or the back of the throat.*

- *Someone with the ability to sing all the notes in the song/s.*

- *Someone with the ability to play the role connected to those songs.*

Remember, this is your opportunity to ascertain range and ability.

REHEARSAL PREPARATION

REHEARSAL PREP FOR THE SINGER

Once you have your cast let them know your expectations before you begin the rehearsal process.

It's often helpful if the cast are familiar with the basic melodies and structures of the songs before the first music call, and as performers have different sets of skills and strengths it is a good idea to provide them with as much learning material as possible.

The ideal set of preparation tools would include:

- *A copy of the sheet music or, alternatively, charts that include the singers' melody lines.*

- *A recording, or link to the recording, of the relevant music. Bear in mind that there are many versions and in various keys and delivered in different styles. Try to choose one that is close to the style in which you will be working.*

- *Playing the specific voice part on the piano and posting it to a social-media group is also helpful, when preparing for rehearsals, particularly for those who are unfamiliar with reading sheet music.*

REHEARSAL PREP FOR YOU

Know the music well!

Know the forms, the cuts, the repeats and the key changes of every song. Play through the individual parts of group numbers before your first rehearsal. You will find that pre-recording voice parts will assist your own preparation greatly.

REHEARSALS

ESTABLISH THE WORK ETHIC

Start as you aim to continue, and then continue as you started. High expectations lead to high returns so begin by establishing boundaries:

- *Set a disciplined tone for rehearsals.*
- *Make sure performers respect each other by keeping quiet and avoiding distractions especially when learning voice parts.*
- *Set goals for each rehearsal and ensure that they are met.*
- *Set goals for each performer for personal work outside of the rehearsal room.*
- *Move forward as scheduled in the next rehearsal.*

FIND THE LEADERS

Select certain cast members to assist you in teaching or rehearsing the required musical pieces. Teenagers, for example, can have more success in motivating peers. And even with an adult cast, having helpers can often mean that voice groups can separate and consolidate harmonies simultaneously rather than one at a time.

Give them a title – e.g. Soprano Group Captain – and a job description and then let them own and fulfil the role.

TEACHING THE MATERIAL

An exceptional teacher once told me that to accommodate the learning styles of all the students in one class, the teacher should teach the same lesson in six different ways. In that spirit, I cover all bases by providing each cast member with all available materials such as sheet music, lyrics, recordings and backing tracks. This allows them to choose their preferred learning format. Other aspects include the following:

- *Note-bashing has its place, but so does responsible learning. If you begin by spoon-feeding your cast, they will come to rely on that.*

- Teach the harmonies to the separate groups and then allow the voice captains to continue with the teaching process. This reduces the rehearsal time and saves you from too much repetition.

- Repetition is vital but this can be done both in the rehearsal room and at home. Your cast should have their individual parts recorded and/or written down in their sheet music.

- Music is often 'learned' overnight, by unconscious assimilation. Do some serious note-bashing, but know that the fruits of your efforts will probably only be seen in the next rehearsal.

- Set deadlines for the cast to know sections, and ensure that your voice captains are, at every given opportunity, rehearsing those in their harmony groups.

- Where possible, encourage cast members to record harmonies on their mobile phones.

SOLOISTS

Spend time in private rehearsal with your soloists. Encourage them to mark their sheet music with any notes you give them on diction, dynamics, accents and style. It may take time for their voices to settle into their song/s, so be patient and encouraging. Above all, build their confidence.

Remember, we hold stress and tension in our necks, and therefore, our throats. If your performers trust you and are relaxed, you will get the very best out of them.

TO TRANSPOSE OR NOT TO TRANSPOSE?

It is true that changing the key of a song can change the feel. Jazz numbers, for example, work better in flat keys (Bb, Eb, etc.) because those keys have a more mellow sound. It is also true that the composer of a musical has arranged the songs, not just as separate pieces, but as musical milestones that work together to produce one integrated journey. Interfering with keys can interrupt the flow of that journey.

Having acknowledged that, I believe there are instances where a key can and perhaps *should* be transposed:

○ *If you have found your leading performer in every respect, but their solo songs are a tone outside of their range.*

○ *If the singer is wobbling precariously between chest and head voice. Sometimes even a semitone up or down will mean that they can sing strongly and comfortably.*

○ *If young voices are being strained.*

CHORUS

Singing in a chorus is a skill acquired through a disciplined rehearsal process. You may end up feeling like a sergeant major, but attention to detail will bring the smooth, homogenous sound you are looking for.

Once they know what they are singing, pay attention to *how* they sing it:

Vocal energy vs shouting: Asking singers to sing with more 'energy' (rather than just louder) helps to lift the level of their vocals without ruining the quality.

Singing with feeling: The performance factor is of the utmost importance! The audience wants to feel something when someone is singing on stage. This requires the performer to connect emotionally with their song/s in order to bring their performance to life. It is important, however, that they do not become overwhelmed by their own feelings and choke up!

Dynamics: The music should take the audience on a journey, particularly an emotional journey containing a series of highs and lows. Dynamics contribute a lot to this! Musical dynamics will bring a song to life, enhancing the melody and lyrics to evoke the desired response.

Mic technique: Obviously this doesn't apply if you are using radio microphones but when using hand-held mics, there is nothing worse than the 'rock-star wannabe' who holds the microphone a metre from their mouth when belting a note. It starts to sound like an intermittent mobile phone signal.

Diction: The audience needs to hear and understand every word that is being sung. Little changes in mouth position make lyrics more coherent and produce a better tone.

Together is better: It's one thing to sing and another to dance, but it's a challenge to sing and dance simultaneously! When rehearsing a musical number, it is best to combine the moves with words (and the musical rests and accents) so that the body and voice get used to working together. Wherever possible, there should be a connection between a word/phrase and dance steps. You will find that combining the two also helps your cast to learn both the lyrics, and the choreography, faster.

FINAL WORD

As a vocal director, the greatest gift you can give your cast members is confidence. Through thorough preparation and positive affirmation, you are giving them the courage to sing out and be heard.

RESOURCES

VOCAL RANGES

Soprano: Highest female voice type. Range approx B3 to C6.

Mezzo Soprano: Second highest female voice type. Range approx G3 to A5.

Contralto: Lowest female voice type. Range approx E3 to F5.

Tenor: Highest male voice (unless counter-tenor). Range approx C3 to B4.

Baritone: Most common male voice. Range approx G2 to G4.

Bass: Lowest male voice. Range approx D2 to E4.

Range: The notes a singer is able to produce.

Weight: Light voices tend to be bright and agile, whereas 'heavy' voices bring darker, richer tones.

Tessitura: The part of a vocalist's range which is most comfortable to sing.

Timbre: A singer's unique voice quality and texture.

DYNAMICS

Piano: (*p*) Soft.

Mezzo piano: (*mp*) Medium soft.

Pianissimo: (*pp*) Very soft.

Fortc: (*f*) Loud.

Mezzo forte: (*mf*) Medium loud.

Fortissimo: (*ff*) Very loud.

Crescendo: Gradually getting louder.

Decrescendo/Diminuendo: Gradually getting softer.

TEMPO

Allegro: Quick.

Lento/Largo: Slow.

Accelerando: Gradually getting faster.

Decelerando: Gradually getting slower.

A capella: Without accompaniment.

Cantabile: In a singing style.

Da capo: (*DC*) Repeat from the beginning.

Del segno: (*DS*) Repeat from the sign.

Fine: Finish/the end.

Legato: Smooth/joined.

Staccato: Abrupt/separate.

Tutti: Together.

LOOKING AFTER YOUR VOICE

Keeping Healthy

No one wants to hear the leading lady growling her notes or the chorus singing through blocked noses. It is vital that everyone does their level best to stay healthy and avoid colds and flu with particular attention to:

Good rest: With a busy schedule it is vital that you take time to relax and rest.

Healthy eating: Without advocating any 'diet', remember that healthy eating is always beneficial, but even more so when extra energy is needed to perform at our best. Nutritionally packed, low sugar, and preferably dairy-free meals and snacks are first choice if possible.

Hydration: Drink, drink, drink! Vocal cords love to be kept hydrated with good, old-fashioned H_2O.

Supplements: Vitamin C and ginger are a great combination for warding off colds and flu.

Maintaining the Voice

In the same way that we regularly check our cars' fuel level, oil and water levels and tyre pressure, so we need to keep a careful eye on our vocal health and fitness.

Here are a few points for consideration:

Warm-ups before each show: This is vital! All cast members must warm up together, not only to prepare your voices to be warm for the opening number, but to establish a collective focus.

Avoid cheer-leading: Sports-day screaming is to be avoided at all costs! If necessary, draw on your acting skills and mime the shouting, but do not abuse your vocal cords.

Sensible eating: Watch what you eat:

Dairy and sugar are two no-go foods as they create a lot of unwelcome mucus. The audience doesn't want to listen to a lead singer warble their way through a phlegmy delivery of the show-stopping number!

Anything very spicy is not good for the voice. Reflux can cause swelling of the vocal cords. Swollen vocal cords cannot vibrate which means you will not be able to sing.

If you have to eat before the show it should be a light snack. No one can sing easily with a full stomach putting pressure on the diaphragm.

Keep hydrated with lots of water although preferably not too cold close to a performance. When muscles get too cold they contract and you want your throat muscles to be warm and relaxed.

SOUND

Acoustics: The behaviour of sound. The acoustic of a room depends on its size and shape, as well as the number and position of sound-absorbing and reflecting material.

Amplifier: Sound equipment that amplifies a low-current signal from one source (e.g. mixing desk) into a higher-current signal suitable for driving speakers.

Backing vocals/BVs: Additional vocals for a musical which are performed offstage in an adapted space, pre-recorded or on a click track.

Backline: The basic equipment required by a live band aside from their hand-held instruments.

Click track: Pre-recorded music and/or vocals on one track and a second track which consists of a click used by the MD to keep the live performers and the recorded material synchronised.

Compressor: Sound-processing equipment that evens out unwanted changes in volume, and controls noise and distortion levels.

Feed: Power supply to a piece of equipment.

Headset: A headphone and microphone combination for theatre communication.

In-ear monitors: Small earphones worn by some singers so that they can hear the monitor mix which reduces the number of monitors needed on stage.

Mic: Abbreviation for microphone.

Mixer: A desk consisting of a number of input channels each having its own control channel. Also known as a sound desk.

Monitor: An onstage speaker which allows the performers to hear the output of the PA or the band.

Radio mic: A 'hands-free' microphone used extensively in musical theatre consisting of a small capsule which can be placed in the hairline or taped to the cheek. It is supported by a battery pack usually contained in a belt around the actor's waist.

Rider: A list of specific technical requirements for the production.

Soundscape: A background sound that runs under a scene to help establish atmosphere in the world of the play.

Voice-over/VO: The pre-recorded voice of an actor used for announcements, narration, to indicate a thought process or to cover a scene change.

Chapter Three

CHOREOGRAPHY

Janine Bennewith-Van Wyk

Janine Bennewith-Van Wyk is a multi-award-winning choreographer. Although originally trained in ballet, tap and modern dance, Janine's experience with styles such as pantsula, African jive, contemporary, jazz, Latin, ballroom, adage and freestyle has resulted in extraordinary versatility in both performance and choreography.

Chances are you're a good choreographer and you have a group of talented dancers in your production. This doesn't necessarily mean, however, that your creative vision will be realised! In this chapter there are tips that, if effectively implemented, will raise the standard of dancing in your production.

The first thing you should bear in mind is that you are part of a team. The second thing is that your job is to bring the director's vision to life. Your choreography is just one facet of the whole and you don't want to be the bit that doesn't fit!

The director will have shared their vision with the team at the first production meeting, but make a point of having a one-to-one session well in advance so that you can discuss the production scene by scene.

I love this process because together we will listen to the music, study the set model and scene changes, and throw around ideas until we are both on the same page. It's such an important meeting because by the end of it you should have a very clear idea of the director's expectations for each scene of the production.

If you are working with a far-sighted director, your auditions will be held long before the rehearsals begin. This means you will know the cast you are choreographing for, as well as their capabilities.

THE AUDITION

When holding a dance audition, (particularly with younger performers), patience is key.

The Length: Set about twelve bars of choreography, just enough to see how quickly they catch on and retain the steps. Don't shoot yourself in the foot by setting too much. The quicker they can learn the routine, the quicker they can perform it and the quicker you can assess them.

The Level: Set the audition piece at the level at which you intend to continue. If the choreography is too easy, it could result in a show stuck at that level. Too difficult and you run the risk of undermining confidence before you have even begun. Aim for an intermediate level. This will immediately reveal the dancers who would struggle to realise your choreography.

The Pace: Bear in mind that auditions are already daunting, so avoid intimidating the auditionees further by racing through the routine. Teach at a fairly slow pace but resist spoon-feeding. Once you are confident that they know the steps, stand back and watch.

Make it clear to the performers that you do not have a crystal ball and despite any promises of *'When I'm on stage...'*, you can only assess what they show you. Similarly, you must remind yourself that you do not have a magic wand to transform a non-dancer into a dancer. Remember, your choreography is only as good as the performers you choose at the audition, and you will always have to choreograph to the level of the least able.

PREPARATION

'5,6,7... er...'

Many of us have worked for 'that choreographer' who takes hours to set sixteen bars. It's a better use of time to pre-choreograph and then be flexible enough to change or enhance your work once you see it come to life.

RESEARCH

The foundation to any creative process is to do your homework.

Watch footage of anything choreographed in a similar style to the one necessary for your production. Watch as much as you can until you are saturated in the style. This will trigger your own creativity and then you can begin.

Don't copy choreography! By all means watch it and study it, until you understand the genre, but don't plagiarise the work of other choreographers!

Feel: Close your eyes and allow the music to speak to you.

Listen: Hear the different instruments in the piece. Are there syncopated beats you can add steps to? Are there swirling violins that remind you of pirouettes?

ROUSING RHYTHM

Because of my background in tap dancing, I listen to all the rhythms and cross-rhythms and add steps that accentuate some of those rhythms, and then adapt them to the style of the dance I am choreographing. This works well when choreographing for a big cast as you can divide them up into 'instruments'. Each group may have a different rhythm and step but it all comes together, just like the instruments do in the music. Be aware that you cannot do this for the entire number or the audience will get dizzy.

Broad strokes: Understand the story you are trying to tell in a particular dance and mark out the beginning, middle and end.

Fine strokes: Break the music down into bars and set each bar individually.

Dance: Unless it's a cameo moment for a 'specialist' performer, do not choreograph something that you yourself cannot do! You may have amazing visions in your head, but you must be sure that they are physically possible before making your performers attempt them.

Design: It's not just about a series of individual steps, it's also about the pattern/s of the group. Sometimes patterns are difficult to pre-choreograph as it's hard to imagine thirty people in front of you and the various positions they take on the stage. Avoid keeping the same pattern throughout the number. This is where you can play and be creative!

Traffic: This refers to the movement of the performers. Always move them around the performance space in varied and artistically pleasing patterns.

REHEARSALS

Where the fun really begins!

Space: Make sure your performers are rehearsing in a space that is similar to the stage space. There's no point in allowing them lots of space in rehearsal and then expecting them to reduce everything by half once on stage. All the movements will already be fixed in their muscle memory and it will be difficult for them to adapt.

Order: Unless there is a very valid reason for doing so, start from the top of the show and work your way through to the finale.

Schedule: Stick to the schedule. You do not want to use all your time on Act One and then find you have no time to rehearse Act Two. This puts an enormous amount of pressure on everyone. Always aim to finish the number in the given time even if it looks like a train wreck! As long as the cast remember the steps, you still have time to make them look good.

The Iron Fist in the Velvet Glove: Be firm but gentle with your performers. Do not accept the word 'can't'. First, we try, and if we do not succeed then we will change it. But be fair. Never give a performer steps that are beyond their expertise. It will make them look awkward.

TEACHING YOUR CHOREOGRAPHY

Try to build your performers esteem from Day One:

Adapt: You may have to change some of your choreography. Often I will be halfway through teaching a routine and the director will politely explain, 'She won't be able to do that as she has a massive hat on, and her frock is huge!' Okay! So take a minute to re-think it – find a different way. Once you have used your 'adapt-on-the-spot' muscle a few times, quick adjustments will become easier.

Be patient: Allow time for the choreography to sink in.

Polish: Allow time for clean-ups – e.g. following through with arms, heads in the same direction, completing steps, and so on.

Showcase strengths: It's very important to know your dancers' capabilities so that you can play down each individual's weaknesses and enhance their strengths. So, for example, if you have a dancer who is brilliant at turns, include it as a quick solo. It will only take up two counts but will add a little feature to your number.

Encourage: Performers will always work harder when they feel good about themselves.

Don't overthink what you have set. You can tweak any choreography that may not be working for whatever reason, but constantly changing steps is counter-productive.

THE FINAL WEEK OF REHEARSALS

Once your cast have learned the choreography for the entire show, go back and clean each number. Brace yourself! This is a painful procedure for everyone involved but it has to be done.

It is best to work in sections. Run through about quarter of the song then tell them and show them what it should look like. Go from the top and repeat that section until they are in time with one another, their spacing is correct, their arms are doing the same thing, their heads turning the same way, their legs at the same height and everyone is facing the front when necessary. Then do the same with the next section and the next, until they are able to perform the entire number as a polished piece.

Despite being somewhat tedious, this process brings the greatest reward as it raises the level of performance – and the choreography comes to life.

PRODUCTION WEEK

The director will have scheduled a placing call and you will be given the opportunity to ensure that all dancers are hitting their marks and are spaced correctly.

All the work you did in clean-up week will look as though it is lost when you get into the theatre. The change in location, being on set, with costumes, sound and lighting will all contribute to a sensory overload which can be disorientating.

After you've taken a deep breath, gently take the cast through the placing call and remind them that the space is no different to how you rehearsed it in the studio. Then, just be patient. They will find their feet.

Once the dress rehearsals begin, only stop and fix something if absolutely necessary for safety. Otherwise let the numbers run. It's the only way to allow all the elements to sink in. Sit in the auditorium and take notes that you can share with the cast either after the rehearsal or before the next rehearsal, which is sometimes better as the cast don't absorb much when they're tired. Keep encouraging and polishing until opening night. Then, it's over to them.

FINAL WORD

Regardless of age, all performers should be treated with respect. Believe me, they will respect you in return. Find the balance between pushing them and being patient and never forget that you are pushing them to a place of vulnerability. They have to trust you.

Once they see that you are bringing them to a level of excellence that they would not be able to achieve on their own, they will blossom.

RESOURCES

TERMS

Accent: The dominant beat of a measure of music. Usually the first beat in a bar.

Ad lib: To improvise. (Used in 'freestyle' dancing.)

Canon: A movement beginning with one person and repeated by subsequent individuals in turn.

Choreography: The design of a dance piece including sequences of steps, patterns and movements.

Choreology: The notation of dance movement.

Echo: An individual or group performs a movement which is repeated by a second individual or group.

Embellishment: A detail added to a basic movement.

Floorwork: Dance movements performed lying down, kneeling or sitting.

Genre: A specific form of dance characterised by specific movement conventions.

Improvisation: Spontaneous, unplanned, un-choreographed movement.

Mirroring: Movements performed in mirror image to one another.

Motif: A movement or gesture that can be developed or elaborated on within the choreography.

Narrative structure: Choreography that tells a story.

Phrase: A series of movements linked together to form a distinctive pattern.

Repetition: The repeat of a movement.

Rondo structure: A recurring section which alternates with contrasting sections (ABACADA).

Sequence: A series of phrases.

Style: a) A sub-division of a genre – e.g. Within the genre of ballet there are classical and contemporary styles.

b) The individual style of a dancer or choreographer.

Tableau: A still picture or shape created by performers.

Unison: The same movements at the same time.

Chapter Four

PRODUCTION DESIGN

Greg King

A multi-award-winning set and costume designer,
Greg King has worked on countless productions
in a wide variety of venues. His name has become
synonymous with innovation and excellence.

Just as the actors communicate to their audience with voice, movement and expression, the design of a show is a visual language which uses space, structural form, layout, colour and stylistic rendering to communicate feelings, moods and ideas which support the director's vision for the show.

Rather than explaining how to paint a backdrop or build a staircase and so on, I have tried to present some ideas and pointers to help you think outside the box and to come up with a production design that is practical, affordable and blows everyone away with your amazing creativity!

We're going to examine these seven starting points:

- *Serving the script and the playwright's storytelling.*
- *Serving and supporting the director's vision/interpretation of the script.*
- *Re-thinking the venue.*
- *Picking out the information you most wish to emphasise and communicate through your design.*
- *Giving the production its own visual identity.*
- *Making and meeting the deadlines of the production schedule.*
- *Coming in on, or (even better) under budget.*

THE SCRIPT

Rule number one: the script should be your bible.

All your design choices, no matter how simple or technical, should be made to support the telling of the story as clearly and creatively as possible.

- *Read and re-read the script.*
- *Read it again.*
- *Make a synopsis: a list of the scenes in the show. There may already be one at the front or back of the script. Then make a list of all the major events in each scene, particularly ones that involve the*

set. List all the entrances and exits, what structural features and furniture are required for actors to work on. If there are multiple scenes, which ones are most important, or used the most?

○ *While you're at it, make a props list too, if this is your responsibility.*

SCENE CHANGES

One of the big challenges for a designer is a show with scene changes. This not only involves creating several different looks for the stage, but also the nightmare of where and how to store everything offstage. It is critical to consider how these scenic elements are arranged onstage and backstage to make the transitions from one scene to the next practical and efficient. Every performance space has its own storage limitations, but these often lead to the most exciting creative discoveries.

In these cases, less is usually more. It is often best to create a unit set with multiple acting spaces and levels, with a few scenic elements that can be moved on and off to indicate a change in location if necessary. This will also save long and complicated scene changes which hold up the action. (Lighting can do this effectively too.)

Try to identify which scenic elements could be used more than once. Often a few simple changes can indicate a change of location rather than a whole scene change.

As an example, in Yasmina Reza's play '*Art*', the action jumps quickly between three different apartments of the three characters. The original set design by Marc Thompson was a neutral white box with three chairs, each one telling us something about each of the characters: A classical curvy one, a very modern one with clean sharp edges, and a comfy armchair. They were all upholstered in white so they looked like they belonged together. The only thing that changed was the lighting, and a single painting on the back wall which indicated which apartment we were in.

COSTUME DESIGN

Costumes are an integral part of the production design as a whole. We'll talk about costume later, but if this is also your department, now is a good time to create a costume plot. This is a table which lists all the scenes in the play along the top line, and a list of characters (including each member of the chorus/ensemble) down the left column. As you read the script, fill the table with what each character should be wearing in each scene. This will give you an instant reference to the number of costumes required, if there are quick changes required and which items can be sourced and which will require making.

If someone else is the costume designer, make sure you compare notes! The set and costumes must complement each other. A bright red backdrop plus bright red costumes equals invisible performers.

THE DIRECTOR

Hold a meeting with the director. Understand their vision or concept for the show. The director may well want to put their own personal stamp on the show; for instance, by modernising a Shakespeare play to emphasise that its themes or message is relevant to modern audiences, or setting it in a different period to show how history repeats itself. He or she may wish to localise it to make it more accessible or to make its humour stand out. All of these choices will have a direct impact on how you style the production. You may have had such brilliant ideas yourself and this is also your opportunity to suggest such things to the director to formalise a creative concept and vision for the show.

THE VENUE

Visit the venue. Spend some time, preferably alone, in the space with your thoughts. Ask yourself if this is the best space available for presenting your show.

Remember, halls are not theatres! Sometimes I think that being asked to put on a production in a community or school hall is like asking the first rugby team to play their best game on a netball court. Just as grass and some white lines don't make a rugby field, neither do a raised stage, chairs and some velvet curtains (that hopefully still open and close) make it a theatre! Is there an alternative that is available to you? Sports venues can sometimes serve your production better than the mouldy old hall, and you'll be applauded for your originality before you've even designed anything!

However, always think about how the space will serve or influence the play. *A Midsummer Night's Dream* might work better in gardens, or *Winnie the Pooh* in the park across the road.

How cool would it be to do *Romeo and Juliet* in a school quadrangle, where there are already stairwells and balconies and enough open space to choreograph some thrilling fight sequences? If this is a school production, perhaps the entire play could be about two rival schools, or two feuding gangs within a school. There's a whole production concept right there! (Costumes definitely sorted!)

What about a production of *The Little Mermaid*, *Treasure Island* or *The Odyssey* in and around the school swimming pool?

Of course, alternative venues come with their own problems:

○ *Can you set up suitable and sufficient seating for your audience?*

○ *Can your performance area be effectively lit?*

○ *Are there dressing rooms nearby?*

○ *Are there toilets for cast and audience?*

○ *If you're outdoors, what about the weather? Is it the rainy season, is there a back-up plan, like an extra night on which the show can be rescheduled?*

So you've thought all this through, got really excited, had your bubble burst, and returned to the boring old hall.

But the brain storming isn't over. Who said you have to perform on the stage? What possibilities abound if you turned everything around?

The double doors at the back, or the gallery, or just the open floor space might inspire all sorts of dramatic possibilities.

How would the show work if you did it in the round, with seating arranged on all four sides, and the acting space in the middle?

This kind of set-up creates an intimacy with an audience that is great for drama, and choreography becomes a whole new ball game. Considering these options may again inform your production concept.

YOUR DESIGN

Study the action and the characters in each scene. In most cases, the design will immediately tell the audience about the context in which the play or a particular scene is taking place. This not only refers to what kind of environment they're in, but also the period and the location of this place. But it can also give the audience clues about the characters themselves, their tastes, their social and financial status, their relationships, their moods and psychological states.

If the place belongs to a particular character, consider how they have chosen to decorate their environment. The dressing of the room can give the audience a whole lot of information about the character who owns that space, before they have even said a line.

You can also give status to a particular character by arranging the furniture in a way that puts them in a position that informs the audience of their status in the scene. The king's throne placed centre stage on a raised rostrum will give him maximum status. But if the scene is about a wicked witch crashing the party to curse his newborn child, then a doorway for her to burst through would be a far better use of that prominent position, especially if it was backlit by a dramatic sky!

So you see, by studying the action of the scene, and the characters in it, you can pick out the information you most wish to communicate and emphasise through your design.

VISUAL IDENTITY

Literal or abstract? That is the question.

In many cases, productions for young people will be presented in a realistic or naturalistic style. In these instances, the designer will set out to render a literal setting or location that is either completely realised or suggested with a few key scenic elements. These need to be carefully chosen and presented in a way that will best inform the audience about the context of the scene.

Ask yourself: 'Is everything there necessary?'
'Is everything necessary there?'

This is a great rule of thumb to ascertain how each visual choice is either adding value or distracting from the intention of the scene.

But there are many other stylistic approaches to designing a show. Instead of creating a literal space, a more abstract setting may express the mood or emotional context of the play or a particular scene.

It's all about the visual language you choose for your production. The best examples of these may be found in the contemporary designs of classic operas which are well-known by audiences, and which have been explored, excavated and reinterpreted by creative directors and designers, to reveal their deeper emotional or psychological truth.

COSTUME DESIGN

Many of these ideas and approaches inform the visual identity of your costume design as well. In everyday life we can assume so much about a person from the way they dress. On stage the same principle applies: costumes can give the audience visual clues about each character's status, class, culture, the period they are living in, and their personality.

Costumes can also be cut and styled to accentuate an actor's physical features which are suited to the role they're playing. If you're doing *Grease,* don't give Danny any old T-shirt to wear. Find a slim fit that accentuates his upper body so that he can strut with macho confidence. If you're doing *Snoopy,* dress your cast in slightly oversized clothes that make them all look smaller, like young children.

The costumes can also communicate ideas about relationships between characters. In *West Side Story* the grungy street gear of the Jets can stand out in strong contrast to the flashy Latino colours worn by the Sharks. When Tony and Maria are together, you could subtly emphasise this contrast to suggest that their love is doomed, or find a way to make them match to indicate that they belong together. The choice is yours, depending on how you want to make the audience feel.

Costumes can also be designed to give your production a visual identity and communicate its moods and tone. Costumes for a pantomime for young audiences ought to have a bright, cartoon-like quality, unlike a drama even if it is set in the same period. You may also choose a particular colour palette for all the costumes, which makes a statement about all the characters in the show, rather than focusing on each one's personal identity.

Be careful when using colour to be symbolic. Colours mean different things to different people. Purple might suggest royalty to you, but to others it might look funereal. Red might mean passion to one person, but for someone else it says danger. Colours also mean different things in different cultures. White suggests purity, virginity and peace in Western culture, but in some Eastern cultures it symbolises death.

SCHEDULING

Regular meetings and communication with your director and the stage and/or production manager are critical to make sure that all deadlines are carefully scheduled.

A production meeting with all the members of the production team should be held well ahead of the first rehearsal to make sure everyone is aware of one another's needs and intentions. At this meeting a presentation of the set design is usually expected.

COMMUNICATING YOUR DESIGN

Although computer technology offers a number of ways of creating and presenting amazing three-dimensional designs, I still find that a physical scale model of the set is the best way to communicate your intentions as designer. The model is a useful reference in the workshop if there are carpenters and artists who are bringing your design to life, and especially in the rehearsal room where the director and actors are having to imagine the space in which they will be performing.

Rehearsals will usually begin with a first read-through of the script with the full company. It is at this meeting that a presentation of the model will give all the performers a clear idea of what to expect when everything eventually comes together.

If rehearsals are taking place off-stage it is extremely helpful for the director and actors if you can mark out the layout of the set on the floor with masking tape. This will give them an idea of the size of the performance space, the position of entrances, levels, steps, and so on, so that there are no surprises when they get on stage.

If you are doing a show with multiple scenes, use different coloured electrical insulation tape to indicate the position of the different scenery for each scene. The floor mark-up is usually the stage manager's responsibility if you have one, but in any case they will need an accurate ground plan from the designer, with all the relevant measurements.

PROPS

If props are the designer's responsibility, there may also be dates in the rehearsal schedule where necessary props or scenic items are required in the rehearsal room for the actors to work with. Again, regular communication with the director or stage manager is necessary for you to stay on top of these deadlines.

SET-UP

When you eventually get on stage, there ought to be a technical schedule created by the stage manager that gives every department sufficient time to deliver.

The first period of the set-up is usually dedicated to putting up the set. Even if you are not physically responsible for getting the set on stage, as the designer you ought to be present to troubleshoot any issues and ensure that your design is set up according to everyone's expectations.

When everything is in place, the lighting department can focus lights, the sound department can rig monitors and microphones, and the actors can come in and start working. But it is important that everything practical is set up first.

All moving scenery must be functional, so that everyone knows what goes where. Dressing decorating and finishing touches can come later.

I have learned (the hard way) that nothing should be added after the final dress rehearsal. That extra vase of flowers might not leave room on the table for the tea tray, or that additional draping might completely block the view for part of the audience. Actors can be distracted and so anything that suddenly appears on opening night could bring the show to a crashing standstill!

BUDGET

Consider your resources. One of the biggest challenges for a designer is having to make miracles on a really tiny budget. I always begin by looking at what already exists. Any school or company that has put on a show before is bound to have a stash of stuff created for previous productions. The more that can be refurbished, recycled and reused, the better, and whatever budget is available can then be used on decorative detail.

Don't limit yourself to what's in the scenic store. Is there other unusual stuff lying around that can be put to good use? Back in high school we did a production of *The Wizard of Oz.* All the woodwork benches from the technology department were placed end-to-end down the centre of the hall to make a fabulous Yellow Brick Road which ran through the audience.

We also did a production of *The Jungle Book* for which we found some old scaffolding that had been used to paint the hall. By arranging it in a creative way, we built a wonderful jungle gym that made a great set for our show, with multiple levels and opportunities for tumbling and physical stunts and tricks.

As with the performance space itself, the materials that are most readily available to you may lead you to an entire visual concept for the production as a whole. Very often, the things that start out as limitations can guide or inspire you to create a totally original design.

In the same way, using found materials to dress or decorate a set can define your creative concept. An underwater setting could be made entirely out of bubblewrap, or a garden created from newspaper with origami flowers. With a little imagination, possibilities are boundless.

You should also consider the skills of the people who might assist in constructing your brilliant design. This might lead you to presenting your show in a completely original way...

In all of these cases, however, it's important that you come back to the script, and the playwright and the director's intentions. Does all this wonderful creativity respond to those intentions? An exciting visual opportunity can just as easily be a distraction, or do your production a disservice if it does not serve the show as a whole.

FINAL WORD

The possibilities are endless. It's all about marrying the creative intention with the resources that are readily available to you. It just takes imagination backed by a little organisation.

RESOURCES

SETS & PROPS

Backing flat: Scenic piece that covers an opening in the set – e.g. window or doorway.

Book flat: Two flats hinged together on the vertical edge so that they can be free-standing. Often used as backing flats.

Border: Narrow, horizontal masking piece made of either cloth or flattage that masks the lighting rig or scenery from the audience.

Cyclorama (or Cyc): The rear wall of the stage.

Flat: Lightweight scenic frame covered with scenic canvas or plywood.

Legs: Narrow, vertical masking pieces.

Proscenium arch (or Pros): The frame through which the audience sees the performance.

Raked stage: A stage that slopes down towards the audience.

Revolve: A turntable built into the stage floor, which can be electrically driven or manually rotated.

Set dressing: Items on set that are not used by the performers but add a sense of reality to the set – e.g. pots and pans hanging in a kitchen, curtains, etc.

Skip: A large wicker basket or a box, generally on wheels, for costume and prop storage.

Strike: To take down the set and remove it.

Tabs (or House tabs): The front curtains.

Tech: Abbreviation for 'technical rehearsal'.

Thrust: A type of stage which projects into the auditorium with audience seated on three sides.

Truck: Wheeled platform on which a scene or part of a scene is built and wheeled on.

COSTUMES

Costume fitting: First meeting between the actor and their costume. An opportunity to see if all movement is possible and to adjust the fit if necessary.

Costume plot: Each character's scene-by-scene costume inventory with detailed breakdown of each item.

Dressing rooms: Changing rooms containing rails, mirrors and lights.

Gondola: Enclosed and easily transported costume rail for large quantities of costumes.

Quick change area: Allocated changing area close to the stage, with rails, mirrors and lights.

BASIC PRINCIPLES OF COSTUMING

Colour: What colours are you looking at and why? Which characters need to be in warm colours and which need to be in cool colours? Do you want your costumes to contrast with or reflect the colours in your set? Make sure that there's enough of a contrast for your characters to be seen against the set. Make sure you understand the different effects of lighting on the fabrics you have chosen – e.g. purple will change to brown in amber light.

Period: Are the costumes true to the era in which the production is set? Stay true to the period in shoes, hats and accessories too. You may want to play with the period a little – e.g. authentic period outfits in modern colours.

Practicality: Consider what the character is expected to do. It's unfair to dress a character in a thick, heavy and inflexible costume if they are performing high-energy dance numbers. Make sure the costume sits comfortably on the performer so that they don't have to keep pulling it back into place. The character's shoes should be worn in all rehearsals. This goes for any costume parts that will affect movement.

Chapter Five

PUPPETS & PROPS

Peter Court

Peter Court is the founder and one of the creative geniuses behind the innovative production company Creative Madness. He is an award-winning actor, puppeteer, production designer and director.

This chapter aims to help you to think outside of your usual patterns and consider using puppets and props in innovative ways, and how to use them on stage in conjunction with live actors.

Regardless of the type of production you are staging, puppets can be introduced either as a way of realising a difficult scene or to create a particular character or effect.

One of the ways I use puppetry on stage (apart from creating actual puppet shows) is a technique I call *Minituarism*. Using this technique, I stop the action with the live actors and move the audience's attention to a smaller version of the same scene, continuing the action with puppets. Why? Because, by making the entire scene smaller, you are able to depict large-scale action!

Examples:

- *Characters travelling across a huge distance.*
- *An explosion in a restaurant.*
- *A moment of magic.*
- *Someone flying.*
- *An inner reflection, like a dream... and so on.*

Added benefits are:

- *You can save a lot of money on special effects.*
- *You can save hours of precious rehearsal time.*
- *It can add hugely to the theatrical experience of the audience.*

A QUICK HISTORY LESSON

Puppets are one of the oldest forms of theatre. Prehistoric people probably sat around the fire telling tales, noticed the flickering shadows cast by the flames onto the cave walls and used these magical pictures to enhance and illustrate their stories.

In Asia, puppets were permitted to perform in public when human actors were not. Puppets were also used to explain the mysteries of the Bible to the largely illiterate congregation in European churches. That was back in the days when the Mass was in Latin, a language understood only by the educated. The word 'marionette' actually means 'little Mary.'

TYPES OF PUPPETS

There are really only three types of puppets:

- *Those worked from above*
- *Those worked from below*
- *Those worked from behind*

PUPPETS OPERATED FROM ABOVE

These are:

- *Marionettes*
- *Reverse-Rod Puppets*
- *Sicilian Puppets*

Marionettes: These are operated by strings. A control bar or hand-grip is held in front of the manipulator's body, and the puppet is suspended below this control with thin strings connected to each limb. The puppet body is made to be floppy and fully articulated. This type of puppet is graceful but very difficult to control. The strings tangle easily and the strings get caught on everything. However, they are good if you need to make three or more characters act as a chorus – i.e. doing the same thing at the same time.

Reverse Rod Puppets: These are controlled from above with steel rods attached to a handle or grip control. Each limb is manipulated with a separate steel rod. This type of puppet is slow-moving and can become quite heavy.

Sicilian Puppets: Like marionettes, Sicilian puppets are floppy and fully articulated and controlled from a control bar. The main difference is that the head and body are controlled with steel rods and the arms with strings. The legs (if any) are free-hanging and controlled by twisting the hand control and moving it forward at the same time. This type of puppet is a bit clunky but less likely to tangle. Traditional Sicilian puppets were made of wood, were dressed in armour, and performed battle scenes and fights.

PUPPETS OPERATED FROM BELOW

These are:

- *Glove or Hand Puppets*
- *Rod and Glove Puppets*
- *Rod Puppets*
- *Moving Mouth Puppets*
- *Marot Puppets*
- *Giant Puppets*

Glove or Hand Puppets: The hand slips into a tube shape and becomes the body of the puppet. (The puppeteer's wrist being the puppet's waist.) The first finger goes into the head and the third finger and thumb slip into tubes to control the arms.

Rod and Glove Puppets: These are similar to glove puppets but the head and neck of the puppet is connected to a short rod that is held in the palm of the puppeteer's hand. This rod is controlled by the third, fourth and little finger, allowing the head to turn. The thumb and first finger control the arms and hands. Both of these types of puppet can easily pick up and use small props (buckets, handkerchiefs, brooms, etc.). In performance these puppets are fast, funny and easy to control.

Rod Puppets: These have a head, a torso and articulated arms. A rod (sometimes with additional controls for head movement, eyes, etc.) runs through the body to control the head, and two separate rods control the hands. In performance these puppets are slower and more graceful.

Moving Mouth Puppets: These puppets have rods to control the hands and arms, and the puppeteer's hand goes through the body to control the mouth of the puppet. Moving mouth puppets are held next to the puppeteer's body or high above the head. Most puppets seen on television are of this type.

Marot Puppets: Closely resembling a medieval jester's sceptre, this puppet is simply a head on a stick. It may have a torso and free-hanging arms like a rod puppet without controls. They are very simple but have little theatrical use. If you do figure out how to use one effectively in your production, please let me know!

Giant Puppets: These are constructed onto a backpack to support the weight of the body and head. The puppet's arms are controlled by the puppeteer's hands with long rods. The puppeteer's legs become the legs of the puppet.

PUPPETS OPERATED FROM BEHIND

These are:

○ *Shadow Puppets*

○ *Bunraku Puppets*

○ *Body Puppets*

○ *Object Manipulation*

Shadow Puppets: These are flat, thin, two-dimensional puppets, which may be very simple cut-outs or articulated as required and cut from any thin, light material (card, plastic, plywood, etc.). Limbs can be cut separately and attached to the body with split pins, dental floss or thin wire.

Bunraku Puppets: These are fully articulated figures controlled by toggles or handles attached to the puppet at the back of the head, between the shoulders and at the back of the hips. Hands are controlled with a rod extending backwards from the hand through the wrist and out through the puppet's elbow. The puppeteer holds this rod to articulate the hands and arms. The feet and legs can be free-hanging or controlled by handles at the ankle. Bunraku puppets originated in traditional Japanese theatre and are wonderful for large groups as they require two or three puppeteers per puppet. Lots of practice is needed to get the puppeteers to work together successfully.

Body Puppets: These puppets are really a type of costume. The puppeteer climbs into the puppet, controlling the head with one hand and one of the arms with another. The puppet's free arm is attached to the body at the hand or wrist to stop it from swinging about or, if the hand is weighted, connected with a thin thread from the wrist, up through the neck of the puppet and down to the other wrist of the puppet controlled by the puppeteer. This makes the arm move every time the controlled arm does, giving it life instead of it just hanging. Great fun for fantasy creatures and strange characters.

Object Manipulation: Any object can be moved and manipulated to give it life or character. Add rods or handles if required. This is great for magical or supernatural effects. (I once used broken china dolls to portray the fairies in *A Midsummer Night's Dream*.)

PUPPETEERS HIDDEN OR IN FULL VIEW

Puppeteers used to be hidden from view. I believe, however, that allowing the audience to see how something is done, how a puppet is manipulated or an effect is achieved, adds to the magic of theatre. We see how it's done but still accept it as real, only adding to our willing suspension of disbelief. Also, not having to hide the puppeteers saves on set design and budget!

ADAPTABILITY

All the methods of puppet construction also apply to the making of any props. Whether you are making old-fashioned telephones, Roman soldier shields, vases of flowers, fake wedding cakes or a pet bunny rabbit, the basic methods and techniques remains the same.

So, with that in mind...

CONSTRUCTING PUPPETS AND PROPS

There are as many ways of making a puppet. No one way is right or wrong. It depends entirely on:

○ *What your puppet needs to do.*

○ *What you want the finished puppet to look like.*

Before you dive in with various materials, paints and glues, you need to stop, think about it, and ask yourself a few questions. This will help you in the design process, and in the long run save you money and huge amounts of wasted time!

Think about these questions:

○ *What is the style of the production? Naturalistic, stylised, abstract, fantasy...*

○ *What does the puppet need to do on stage? Gaze at the moon, fly, hold things, spit fire...*

○ *What is the character? Human, humanoid, animal, spirit, monster...*

○ *What is the budget? None, very little, some, not bad, a lot...*

○ *What skills do you have? Paint, sew, glue, solder, cut wood...*

With these questions answered, look up images on the internet of the type of character you want. Don't copy someone else's work. It is illegal and unethical, but there may be a costume detail here or an expression there that you can borrow as inspiration. Once you have your research you can then start sketching.

Yes, you can draw... everyone can draw... no one is asking you to be Picasso or sell your sketch for millions, but it will help you keep the idea and basic look of the puppet in mind as you make it!

*Remember: What your puppet needs to do
and how many people you have to manipulate it
is the most important thing!*

MATERIALS

Choose your materials according to your skills! Don't get me wrong, you can (and will) always learn new skills, but if you are used to doing handicraft, work in paper, card and glue. If you are used to sewing, go with fabric, needle and toy stuffing. If woodwork is your thing and you have the tools, carve away! You will, at some point, have to move into a skill-set where you feel uncertain and inexperienced, but begin where you feel most comfortable and confident!

Here is the secret to making all puppets and props: Every material ever invented can be used to make whatever you want! From plastic bottles to scrap timber, from newspaper to neoprene, from feather dusters to foam rubber... it all works if you get the desired effect. Start by looking for shapes that are close to what you're after and go from there. Your imagination is the key!

METHOD 1: FABRIC SCULPTING

If you are used to sewing, this is a very easy method:

- *Start by creating a pattern for your puppet or use an existing toy pattern. There are literally thousands of free doll patterns on the internet.*

- *Adapt the pattern (enlarge or reduce on your printer or photocopier) to suit your character.*

- *Puppets need to move, so sew all the limbs separately and then join them to the body after you have stuffed them. I like to add (clean/new) cat litter as stuffing into the lower arms and legs of my puppets to add a little extra weight, making them easier to manipulate.*

- *Once stuffed, paint any visible limbs, the face, neck and chest with acrylic paint. This is an easy way to add character and protects the puppet (also, because acrylic is a form of plastic, you can wipe it clean with a damp cloth if the puppet gets dirty).*

If you are using an existing pattern, don't make an exact copy but give the character your own spin. Remember that this must be your work and not a copy of someone else's.

METHOD 2: LAYERED PAPIER-MÂCHÉ

Layered papier-mâché is simply paper and glue over a shape or form. If you're not familiar with this ancient method then do yourself a favour, and get familiar. Papier-mâché will be the mainstay of most of your puppet and prop solutions.

O *Make a form (the basic shape of your puppet or prop) out of... anything! Polystyrene, cardboard boxes, toilet roll tubes... it all depends on your design.*

O *Once you have the basic shape, tear newspaper into strips approximately two to three centimetres wide.*

O *Tear across these strips to make squares. Don't ever cut the paper! Torn paper exposes the rough fibres and blends together more easily. Cut edges leave a ridge that's almost impossible to get rid of.*

O *Paint your form with a mixture of PVA glue (polyvinyl acetate, i.e. cold glue or wood glue) and water (approximately two parts glue to one part water).*

O *Place squares of paper onto the form and smooth flat with your damp fingers or paintbrush, overlapping each piece by about 1cm. Cover the entire form with paper and glue in this way.*

O *You can add features (eyebrows, lips, cheeks, etc.) with crumpled toilet paper or twisted newspaper and glue them into place. Use undiluted glue for this.*

O *Give your form a second layer of papier-mâché using a different type of paper – e.g. brown paper – and then a third layer using newspaper again. This way you can easily see that you have covered the form completely, leaving no gaps.*

O *Allow your puppet to dry completely by leaving it overnight or forty-eight hours before painting.*

Papier-mâché can be sanded to make it really smooth, if you want, but I prefer a few small lumps and bumps in my puppets – it adds reality and texture on stage.

METHOD 3: FOAM RUBBER

Most puppets seen on television are made from foam rubber. There are pros and cons to working with this material.

- *It is not the easiest to work with.*
- *The foam does disintegrate over time (although this takes about five years).*
- *It tears easily unless covered.*
- *It's relatively expensive.*

However, it is light in weight which is a huge plus when it comes to making puppets and props. Foam is sold in cubes and sheets at most places that upholster furniture, so if you can find their supplier and collect yourself, you'll cut the cost. Cubes can be carved using kitchen or electric carving knives. *Please be careful: it's very easy to lose a finger.* If you're using sheet foam, you want medium density about 1 or 1.5cm thick.

Don't let the dealer sell you sheet foam measuring 2 or 2.5cm thick. It's too thick and you'll become frustrated. So get the right stuff!

- *Copy the pattern onto cardboard. Keep the pattern. You might need it again.*
- *Trace the pattern onto the foam and cut the pieces out.*
- *Start applying contact glue to both of the surfaces to be glued together and leave to dry for about three minutes before attempting to stick them together.*
- *Learn from my mistakes! Contact glue sticks when it is dry, not when it is wet. If you try to glue the foam together while it is wet you will just create a sticky mess and glue yourself to your puppet in the process.*
- *Once they are dry, firmly pinch the glued surfaces together to create your puppet head.*

- Glue the moving mouth plate into place and paint with aerosol spray paint. Never use wet paint on foam. It absorbs and goes hard. It is a sponge after all!
- Create the body (a simple tube) and the arms in the same way.
- Dress your character, adding hair last.

If you can get rubber solution glue, you could cover the head with it, creating a thin skin for extra strength before painting, or you can cover the head with fabric. Use something with a stretch – fleece or T-shirt fabric, for example.

METHOD 4: FOUND OBJECTS

Depending on the style of your production, found objects can make really interesting puppets and props. For example, broken toys and dolls can take on a really eerie or sinister appearance if well manipulated.

- If you need more articulation than the object naturally has, break or cut it apart then re-join. If necessary, you can reinforce your found objects with wood, wire or papier-mâché to give them extra strength.
- Add control rods or handles to objects using suitable glue (depending on the material of the object) or by drilling through strategic points such as wrists and ankles (the puppet's, not yours).
- Paint or touch up the object if required and start rehearsing with it to look at its possibilities within your production.

REINFORCE!

Bear in mind that your puppets and props have to survive the run of the show. They will get dumped off stage, someone will step on them in the dark, and a limb or two will get wrenched off, either during rehearsals or performance, when one of the cast goes the wrong way! So reinforce them as much as you can.

AS FOR THE PUPPETEER

If you want your puppeteers to be as invisible as possible, dress them in black, long-sleeved T-shirts, gloves, tracksuit pants and a balaclava.

Alternatively, if you want them to integrate with the puppet, you could dress them in similar colours to the puppet design. Remember, you're not trying to fool the audience into *not seeing* your puppeteers. The idea is to create the theatrical illusion of life with your puppet or prop.

Conversely, dressing your puppeteers in bright colours will make your puppeteers stand out and your puppets vanish – the opposite of what you need on stage.

FINAL WORD

When it comes to puppets and props, the only limitation is your imagination and your budget, and you can always find a way to expand the one and reduce the other.

RESOURCES

HOW TO MAKE A RECYCLED ROD PUPPET

Design is simply a process, a simple series of steps for making your dreams a reality. Anything (and I mean anything) can be made with papier-mâché!!

These are basic construction tips that I hope will stimulate ideas of how you can adapt this pattern to create a whole company of characters.

MATERIALS NEEDED

- *30 x 25cm rectangle of cardboard (the side of a box)*
- *Extra cardboard pieces*
- *Newspaper*
- *Sticky tape*
- *Wood (PVA) Glue*
- *Water*
- *Two-litre plastic bottle*
- *Scissors*
- *Craft knife*
- *Paint*
- *Dowel rods (or broken umbrella spokes or chopsticks)*
- *Fabric for clothing (optional)*

METHOD

Take the 30 x 25cm rectangle of cardboard, make sure the 'corrugation' runs from top to bottom, then cut away one quarter to accommodate your hand.

Roll the cardboard into a tight tube. Much easier if the corrugation runs from top to bottom. Let it spring back and use sticky tape to fix it. This becomes the base head and neck of your rod puppet.

Scrunch newspaper from sides to centre, forming a dome. MAKE LOTS!

Sticky-tape the domes into position forming the cheeks, ears, eyes, lips, dome of head, nose... or whatever features you want.

5 Cover the whole thing in a layer of papier-mâché. Mix two parts PVA glue with one part water, and glue small strips of newspaper all over the head until you can't see the cardboard and newspaper features any more. Put it aside to dry... This might take some time depending on where you live and atmospheric conditions.

(OR)

6 Wash and dry a two-litre plastic bottle. Using scissors and a craft knife, cut across the widest part of the bottle and again just below the neck of the bottle (where the plastic becomes thinner). This will be the shoulders of your rod puppet.

7 Slip your puppet head into the 'neck' hole. Check that it's big enough.

8 Cut hands from cardboard and put some sticky tape over the wrist (which will make it stronger). Punch a hole through the tape and the cardboard.

9 Make arms by rolling cardboard tubes (remember those corrugations), and tape them onto string. Punch two holes in the side of the shoulders and tie the string.

10 Paint the head and dress your puppet, or papier-mâché the body to match the head. Add control rods (broken umbrella spokes/chopsticks/dowel rods) to the hands.

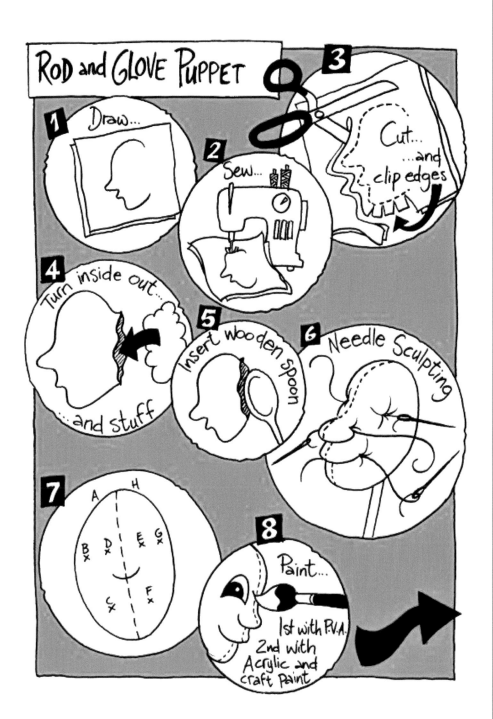

85

TIPS FOR PUPPET MANIPULATION

When you are starting out in puppetry, or wanting to include puppets in your production, most of your time and energy goes into the making of the puppet and the manipulation and performance takes a back-seat. Don't fall into the trap: 'Beautiful puppets. What a shame about the production!' Once you know the type of puppets you are going to be using in your production, get the cast/puppeteers working as soon as possible without the puppet. Use anything to rehearse with – e.g. a tea towel and a tennis ball or toilet rolls on wooden spoons – and follow these basic rules:

LIP SYNCHRONISATION

- *If you are using a moving-mouth puppet, synchronise opening the puppet's mouth with the spoken word. Try not to move the mouth randomly during a sentence.*

- *Don't open the mouth all the way with each word. Try opening the mouth wider on vowel sounds (A E I O U) and only halfway for all the other sounds.*

- *Practise opening the puppet's mouth by moving your thumb downward, without moving your fingers upward. A slight forward thrust of the hand will help. This will help the bottom jaw move and not the top of the puppet's head.*

- *If you're using a puppet that doesn't have a moving mouth, try moving the head as the puppet talks but keep it subtle, don't bounce it about.*

ACTION

Correct action is equal to good puppetry. Make sure to direct your puppets and puppeteers. Puppets rely on action. They look dead if they just stand around and 'talk'. Having said that, remember to suit the action to the words. Don't just let them bob about. A good rule of thumb is to rather let the puppet move each time there is a new thought.

EYE CONTACT

Make your puppets look towards your audience, who need to see the puppet's eyes, body language and expression if they are going to *believe and invest* in the production. The same rules for blocking actors applies to blocking puppets... they are just mini actors after all!

If your stage is raised above the audience, make your puppets look down a little, rather than over the heads of your audience. This will ensure more effective eye contact and credibility. And *always* angle your puppet to 'look' at the person or puppet they are speaking to.

POSTURE

If you want your puppet to look real, you can't ignore their posture. The way an actor holds their body tells the audience a huge amount about their emotional state, whether they're happy, sad, depressed or ecstatic. Think about the posture and how the puppet walks and moves as part of the character. Do they glide? Do they slither or do they galumph about like an oaf?

Unless you've made a decision based on character, always keep your puppets upright. Don't allow them to lean from side to side and never let them lean or slump on the stage.

ENTRANCES AND EXITS

While there are many ways to make a puppet enter or exit, each will be determined by the nature of the scene and the type of puppet:

○ *Puppets operated from above should be dropped in behind a piece of scenery and then walked out in front of the audience. (Unless you want them to appear to be flying, of course.)*

○ *Puppets operated from behind should make a similar entrance or be held upstage of the puppeteer's body and then brought into view as the puppeteer turns to face the audience.*

○ *Puppets operated from below can appear from behind scenery or to make your puppet appear as if they are walking up or down a ramp or stairs. This movement uses the whole arm and the puppeteer must keep their forearm straight, moving it up and down while the wrist is relaxed. The puppeteer moves forward and extends their arm as they bounce the puppet onto the stage. With each bounce of the arm, the puppet comes more fully into view. To exit, do the same in reverse.*

In the beginning, encourage the puppeteers to practise in front of a mirror whenever possible so they can see what the audience is seeing and therefore improve their technique. But don't let them rely on the mirror. It won't be there during the show!

Have fun in both the making of your puppets and in the performance.

Chapter Six

SCRIPTWRITING

Charon Williams-Ros

A multi-award-winning actress, Charon Williams-Ros
began writing scripts in her spare time. She is now in
demand as an established scriptwriter.

This chapter is aimed at all those who find themselves sitting in front of a blank screen (or page), desperately searching for inspiration to write the theatrical society's next show, the annual school production, or even the kayak club's end-of-year extravaganza. The dilemma is the same. You have a few ideas but no solid structure.

There are many excellent, detailed books on scriptwriting, and I would advise any serious writer to read them. (And anyone who takes on writing a play – whether one-act or three-act – is, to my mind, a serious writer.) If you are a first-time writer, or have merely dabbled in scriptwriting before, you could consider writing a musical revue. Songs serve as solid building-blocks in the construction of a production, and you can achieve a level of professionalism fairly easily.

Having said that, please note that regardless of whether your script requires music or not, the ideas in this chapter can translate to most theatrical forms.

You could even use the ideas in this chapter as a creative-writing project to inspire your group, or plan a competition where the winning script is the one you will finally stage.

THE CASE FOR AN ORIGINAL PRODUCTION

Writing your own production makes sense for a number of reasons:

Budget: An original script means you don't have to pay for the rights to perform the piece.

No weak links: You can write for the cast you have and therefore play to their strengths.

○ *If you have one very strong actor and several who are not so strong, you can write a script that favours a narrator, with short sections of dialogue for the other actors.*

○ *If you have one extremely strong singer, perhaps they could narrate in song.*

One of the most satisfying things about writing an original script is the knowledge that your creation will be well within your cast's capabilities.

Universal appeal: Perhaps the most persuasive argument for writing something original is that it's the easiest way to please most people. Our communities are more diverse today than ever before, and an original show provides an opportunity to be completely inclusive.

Authenticity: An original script can often be a better fit for a community, particularly if they live in a unique setting. There are times when the challenge of an established, mainstream production can facilitate growth, and obviously there are human experiences we all share regardless of geography, culture and economic factors, but perhaps your cast would be best served by a script that represents their own stories.

THE MUSICAL REVUE

The musical revue is a type of theatrical entertainment that combines music, dance and sketches. This makes it a popular choice for schools or community theatres wanting to include diverse talent in their productions. They are fun and flexible enough to combine new and established material into one, custom-made package, and you and your team can create something entertaining and/or thought-provoking in a relatively short space of time.

Well-scripted links are important to keep the audience engaged and prevent the production from becoming just another variety show. And providing links instead of a full-length script is within the capabilities of even a first-time writer.

Deciding what theme will hold your musical revue together would be your first consideration. Perhaps you'd like your cast to experience the music of a certain era – e.g. Motown – in which case the vocals, choreography and language should also reflect this genre. Maybe you would rather write a script first and then add a variety of songs with lyrics along the same theme – e.g. A Valentine's show featuring love songs from George Gershwin to Justin Bieber...

Research is the key to creativity. Go online. Type in a couple of keywords and you'll find that there are songs written about every subject under the sun. Reading song lyrics will inspire you further, perhaps even reminding you of other songs, play extracts, or poems, all of which may contribute to your theme.

Be aware that if you are using copyrighted songs (which will be anything written in the last seventy or more years) then you will need to research the situation with rights, seek permission, and possibly pay a fee. In the UK you can find out more information from www.prsformusic.com.

FIRST IDEAS

You can find inspiration all around you.

PARODY

Bring a much-loved but perhaps tired classic book back to life. Or, if yours is a school production, make a set-text novel or play more accessible to teenagers by rewriting the story as a concise modern play or a musical skit with popular songs.

Imagine:

- *A Midsummer Night's Scream*
- *Macbeth the Musical*
- *Jane Eyre rewritten as Jane Air-head*

DÉJÀ VU

Take a famous scene and rewrite it several times in a series of different eras or locations. I once gave this treatment to the balcony scene from *Romeo and Juliet* with hilarious results. Add appropriate music for each location or era and you have all the ingredients for a fun show. (The idea is to look at the scene through a different lens, not mock the original.)

BIOGRAPHY

Tell someone's inspiring life story against a backdrop of music to support that story. Either the lyrics support the story, or the music reflects the era of the person's life. There is a soundtrack to every life, and music which reflects the events and trends of an era will add authenticity to a story. You can use a narrator but flesh out a few scenes with actors as well.

STORY OF AN ERA

Tell the story of a generation. Perhaps your school or organisation is celebrating a significant milestone – e.g. its centenary year – and would like a show to mark the occasion. Find out what was happening in your town, your country, and the world in the year of the school/organisation's origin, and support your story with the behaviour, vernacular, fashions, music and trends of that era.

Time travel is another effective way to tell the story through the eyes of a contemporary.

Bear in mind that whether it's 1920s Charleston music, wartime melodies or protest songs from the '70s, the music and lyrics from any era will provide you with the inspiration for a script and a cast of characters who are impacted by both local and world events.

HIGHLIGHT AN ISSUE

Send a strong message about an important issue by throwing drama, comedy and music at it. For example, if you want to deal with the issue of bullying, consider compiling a collection of the most inspiring stories of people who stood up to bullies from biblical characters – e.g. David and Goliath – to current celebrities like Lady Gaga. Perhaps these stories can be re-enacted and linked together by a group of comic, anti-bullying superheroes.

FAMOUS CHARACTER IN A LOCAL SETTING

What would happen if James Bond came to your town or your school? You could write a comedy depicting any iconic character's encounters with recognisable locals and traditional town events. You could do the same with a well-known celebrity or historical figure. More comedy can be added if the character reveals unexpected qualities – e.g. James Bond's mum keeps calling him.

This also works in reverse: the ordinary character in extraordinary circumstances. Perhaps a local character in an iconic location.

STRANGER THAN FICTION

Read the newspapers. Real-life stories are usually better than anything we can imagine. And if it's local news – even better. You could even use news from within your own group – e.g. *Tuckshop Theft* or *Romance in the Choir*.

CALENDAR-BASED

Any shows relating to a particular day or season – e.g. Valentine's Day, Christmas, Halloween, Summer, etc. – can provide you with a framework for your script. You can add local flavour or you can look at this holiday/celebration through the eyes of an alien.

GENRE, VENUE AND STYLE

The combination of these choices will inform your script. Let's take the two examples from 'Stranger Than Fiction' above:

○ *You've noticed that every member of the choir is in a romantic relationship with another choir member. You could write a romantic-comedy musical in a melodramatic style, set on a choir stand in the school/town hall. With clever use of lighting, you can easily switch from full choir numbers to duets.*

○ *Or the disappearing tuckshop stock? Deciding on a crime caper set outside the tuckshop in the style of an old black-and-white film would give you a great starting point for your script.*

See page 138 for more Genre, Venue and Style ideas.

USE SONGS AS BUILDING BLOCKS

There are a few ways to do this:

Select a variety of songs with a common theme and build a commentary or story around them. Choose a theme that is relevant to your audience, the time of year or the event:

- *If it's a Valentine's show and you choose love as your theme, perhaps build in one or two characters who presume to know a thing or two about love – e.g. Valentino, Don Juan, Freud, Dr Phil, Cupid, or even Romeo and Juliet... and use them as your narrators.*

- *If your theme is travel, perhaps take your audience around the world with a couple of intrepid explorers. You can have a lot of fun with the music, dance and costume of different countries and cultures – e.g.* Around the World in 80 Minutes *or* Two Idiots Abroad.

These are fairly common themes (probably because they work and everybody recognises them), but you could have a lot of fun with unusual themes, such as flying. There are a surprising number of songs about feeling as though you're flying, longing to fly or believing you can fly with or without wings. Throw in a couple of superheroes who can't fly and you have a fun show featuring music from several eras. Of course, if you decide that your theme should just be 'superheroes', flying becomes just one of many other possibilities.

Choose one genre of music and build your story and characters around that music. Here are some examples:

- *Big-band Jazz with ultra-cool, glamorous characters.*

- *Motown Music with strong, stylistic dance moves.*

- *'60s Britpop and fashion explosion.*

You don't have to do the research yourself! Why not give each cast member the responsibility to find one song? Give them a common theme, but perhaps a different era, genre or artist to prevent them all choosing the same songs.

Choose the music of an artist, preferably one who writes songs with strong lyrics, and write a story inspired and supported by the songs. You can do this with any songwriters who have a solid body of work – e.g. George and Ira Gershwin.

This can be adapted to spoken pieces from the works of one author for a non-musical production.

DEVELOPING YOUR IDEA

Taking your ideas to the next level.

WORKSHOPPING A SCRIPT

Workshopping a script is a great way not only to get input from your cast, but also to see immediately what works and what doesn't. Bear in mind, however, that although this may give you access to some of the cast's realities, their initial contributions might be superficial. That's okay. Begin by having an open discussion about what is important to their generation/s and within their community. A good way to access this information is to ask them to bring a song that means something to them. Breaking down the lyrics and discussing them in depth can provide you with profound insights into what is actually going on in their lives, and what they care about.

Once you've established what your cast want to say through this piece, throw a couple of relevant scenarios at them and get them to roleplay.

I've seen this work very well with just a series of monologues and songs. The cast chose their own characters, songs, and wrote their own monologues. The result was a very powerful insight into their realities.

TALENT

Remember, play to your strengths. If you have a group of magicians, write a show that features magic as its main theme. If skateboarding is the local passion, find a way to feature this unique talent. If you are surrounded by singers, include a variation of solos, duets, trios, quartets and ensembles, as well as solos with backing groups. Whatever it is – celebrate it!

PLOT

Who is the protagonist? What do they want? And who or what is stopping them from getting it? Even the most basic of scripts requires more than just smart dialogue. Audiences respond to story, and there is no story without conflict. Even if you are staging a round-the-world musical revue, your lead character needs to have an intention, a reason to be on the trip, and one or more obstacles. Whether they overcome the obstacle or not is up to you, as long as they try.

Obstacles include anything that prevents your character from moving forward. Some examples:

- *A tree across the path*
- *Prison*
- *A magician's spell*
- *Fear*
- *Poor self-image*

They are necessary because they create tension and force your characters to take action, thereby revealing more about them.

CHARACTERS

Adding well-drawn characters to your play will elevate the material. Your principal characters need to be likeable, flawed and engaging. One way to do this is to make them very good at one thing and really bad at something else.

- *A charming but clumsy superhero who knocks out their opponents inadvertently.*
- *Cupid knows which couples belong together, but he has terrible aim and keeps missing his targets.*
- *Adorable Romeo is a terrible kisser.*
- *The brilliant scientist who cannot string two words together in front of a love interest.*

This approach works for your other characters too:

- *A deplorable villain with a great sense of humour.*
- *The alluring but shallow love interest.*
- *The wise mentor who is accident-prone.*

Once you've established your characters, don't leave them there. Show some character development. Your protagonist, in particular, should have been on a journey (literal, psychological, emotional) and learned something by the end of the script.

ARCHETYPES

Numerous books and articles have been written about archetypes, and these are very useful when filling out your cast of characters. Don't just settle for a hero, an ally and a villain. There are mentors, shape-shifters, heralds and shadows, to name a few, who will add colour and life to your script.

While stock characters like the absent-minded professor, the lovable rogue and the dumb muscle are all stereotypes, they do provide a clear basic outline that can be nuanced as you go along.

DIALOGUE

Getting your characters to talk is the fun part! Just remember that each line has to have a reason for being there. These might include:

- *Furthering the plot.*
- *Revealing something about the character.*
- *Hinting at subtext – something going on beneath the surface. Remember, characters very rarely say what they mean.*

Pay attention to how a character speaks. Not everybody sounds the same. Listen to people, watch them; we all have little quirks that reveal something about us. What makes them interesting? Or boring? (One obviously boring character in a group can provide comedic moments.)

Another tip is to speak your dialogue out loud. If you can't get your tongue around it, no one else will.

Most importantly, keep it lean! Too many words will lessen the impact.

TITLE

A clever title will not only give your publicist something to work with, but will inform your audience about the tone of your show.

Perhaps one of your show's songs has a great title that can serve as a title for your production, such as Gershwin's 'Fascinating Rhythm'. Or you can be clever with a famous title by playing with the word order, such as *Juliet & the Romeos*. Attach a one-line description such as:

How many frogs will she have to kiss before she finds her prince?

Within a few words you've communicated that the show is a romantic-comedy.

PACE

How to establish and maintain pace.

THE BEGINNING

Begin by grabbing your audience's attention. Most people do this with a big musical number, but there are several ways to engage an audience from the beginning.

Some of these ideas may appear to be directorial, but the more ideas that originate with you, the more the director has to work with.

Action: Something should be happening from the beginning, something that forces the audience to pay attention.

- *An argument. This works well for a kitchen-sink drama.*
- *A sense of expectancy. Someone's coming. Build the audience's anticipation but make sure it pays off.*
- *A series of interactions. These can be set to music that builds in intensity.*

Sensory Focus: Part of your job as the writer is to focus the audience's attention. One way to do this is to eliminate one of the senses, heightening those which remain.

- *Begin with a blackout. Playing sound alone will cause the audience to listen more intently, particularly if it is a compelling score.*

- *Cut the sound. Mime, or perform as if in a silent film.*

- *Relay the sound from one speaker to another so that it travels around the audience. You can also do this live by placing performers around the auditorium.*

- *Play with dynamics. Begin with the cast whispering, and then gradually or suddenly becoming louder. Or vice versa.*

Surprise!: Do something unexpected.

- *Start the action within the audience. Place a couple of actors in the audience beforehand and, when they take to the stage, it will draw the audience along with them straight into the action.*

- *Reverse the focus. Seat your actors in chairs on stage facing the audience. Which group is the audience now?*

- *Stage a fake issue affecting the audience. This can be anything from parking to health and safety.*

- *A spectacular entrance. These are always fun and needn't rely on expensive special effects. Six to eight cast members could easily carry on your lead character with as much pomp and ceremony as is appropriate.*

- *Mixed media. Because we engage with different mediums in different ways, jumping from one medium to another is a fun way of playing with an audience's expectations. E.g. sound-to-screen-to-stage, or the use of a film or radio broadcast to set your scene.*

- *Stillness. Recreate a famous painting with your actors frozen in a tableau. You can choose to bring them all to life at once or one or two at a time.*

You may even find inspiration for an entire production within one painting as Stephen Sondheim did with *Sunday in the Park with George*, a musical inspired by Georges Seurat's painting 'A Sunday Afternoon on the Island of La Grande Jatte.'

THE MIDDLE

Now that you have their attention, keep it! Whether you are led by the songs or the sketches, you need to establish a flow. This is a way of channelling the energy between your performers and the audience making sure to avoid anything that will interrupt that flow.

Music: If you are not musical, you may need to work with the musical director to choose the right pieces. But, whether you have chosen music based on mood, genre or lyrics, be sure to establish a flow.

- *Vary the tempo and style.*
- *Don't give away too much, too soon. Let the music evolve.*
- *Too many showstoppers will keep stopping the show.*
- *Think about changing the tempo and style of well-known songs to give them new life.*

Narration: Maintain the pace. Keep any narration lean and slick and preferably delivered by an interesting character or characters.

Emotional Journey: You want your audience to feel something, but avoid bashing them around the head with too much of one thing. Build a well-balanced experience with:

- *A bit of drama and intrigue.*
- *A generous helping of laughter.*
- *A heart-stopping moment.*
- *A heart-wrenching moment.*
- *Plenty of pure entertainment.*

Cliffhanger: End the first act with a little bit of intrigue, an unanswered question, a sense of danger, or a promise of things to come. This will guarantee an actively expectant and responsive audience after the interval. Don't disappoint them. Act Two must hit the ground running.

THE END

This is the right place for a real showstopper. Don't allow this final scene or production number to be something just tacked on the end after the resolution. It's always such a pity when a brilliant show fizzles out. You want your audience on their feet applauding, not on their feet sneaking out to the exit. Again, there are many ways to end a show:

Back to the Beginning: End as you began with the world of the production returning to the same stage picture.

- *All the performers return to their original positions in the famous painting (or a different one).*

- *The lead character is carried out again.*

- *You return to a blackout with sound only.*

Save the Best Till Last: Hold something back.

- *A surprise power-house vocalist.*

- *A cameo from the headteacher or director.*

- *The final piece of the puzzle revealed in the final moment. Only one piece, however! Too much dialogue in the final scene will bring your show to a sticky, claggy end.*

- *A plot twist.*

On Its Head: Inverting the reality you've established can be a fun surprise.

- *The narrators are suddenly centre stage and the rest of the cast comment on them, for a change.*

- *If you began with a film clip and you decide to end with one, you could show footage of the audience that you filmed during the show.*

- *The underdog is carried out instead of the lead. Remember, a picture really is worth a thousand words.*

Many revue-devisers use audience participation to bring the show to an end. The idea is that you get the audience dancing, which, in theory, will see them leaving on a high. You could even have the cast dancing through the audience and out of the theatre. Personally, I think it's a *'when in doubt, fade out'* kind of solution, and prefer to see the cast bring the show to an end without relying on the audience to do it for them. Unless your revue is part of a bigger event that will lead to dancing, try to end strongly with a big, musical full-stop.

FINAL WORD

Don't be afraid to write badly. Just write. Don't judge. When you've completed your script, leave it alone for a few days. Then read it. Rewrite what doesn't work. Reassess it at the first read-through. Rewrite the clumsy parts.

Then step back and let the director bring it to life.

RESOURCES

TERMS

Accent: A way of speaking unique to a country or culture.

Act: A large section of a full-length production.

Ad lib: Dialogue in which the actors make up what they say during the performance.

Antagonist: The character who is the opposing force to the protagonist/ hero.

Backstory: Character's experiences that have taken place prior to the action within the play.

Beat: A pause within a scene which might indicate a shift in direction.

Book: The story, dialogue and stage directions (non-musical part) of a musical.

Compilation: A collection of independent scenes or vignettes unified by a central theme.

Conflict: The central drama of a piece. A character wants something but is prevented by one or more obstacles.

Dialogue: The speeches between characters.

Form: A broad category of drama which may contain several styles.

Inner action: The character's thoughts, motivation and intention.

Monologue: One character's extended speech.

Mood: The emotional climate of a scene or moment.

Motif: An image, sound or idea that repeats in order to highlight the theme.

Narrative: An account of linked events.

Protagonist: The principal character whose story is being told.

Realism: Where art impersonates life.

Scene: Smaller sections of an act that take place (usually) in one location and move the plot forward.

Setting: The time and place in which the production is set.

Style: A specific type of drama within a broader form. Also used to describe a distinctive approach to a creative work.

Subtext: The unspoken thoughts or motivations of a character.

Symbol: Something used to represent something else – e.g. A sound to represent death.

Chapter Seven

LIGHTING DESIGN

Tina Le Roux

Tina Le Roux is a multi-award-winning lighting
designer with over twenty-five years' experience
in theatre.

This chapter will introduce you to the crazy, beautiful world of theatre lighting design. Can you juggle? I hope so, because 'Lighting Designer' (LD) is a broad term describing several jobs rolled into one.

O *Artist: The LD is not dissimilar to a fine artist, except our paintbrushes are the lighting fixtures and our canvasses are stages and actors.*

O *Accountant: There's a production budget. It must be obeyed.*

O *Technician: LDs must understand how it all works – from computers, to lighting desks to the lights themselves.*

O *Maintenance Manager: Having the practical ability to fix things and solve practical problems logically and calmly.*

O *Mountaineer: Heights involved!*

O *Comedian: A sense of humour goes a long way!*

O *Inventor: Someone with the ability to think outside of the usual parameters.*

Now throw these qualities into the mix:

O *Nerves of steel: LDs must have the ability to remain calm under pressure.*

O *Patience: You are working with artistic temperaments after all.*

O *Attention to detail is vital!*

O *Adaptable: The needs of each production are different. What works in a dance production may not work in a drama.*

O *Flexible: Someone who enjoys working odd and often long hours.*

O *A good leader: You must be able to make decisions.*

O *A team player: Working towards the same goal as the actors, set designer, crew, stage manager and director.*

Theatre lighting designers work in collaboration with a director, set designer, costume designer, sound designer, lighting crews, riggers, programmers – and a stage management team to create a world on stage and bring it to life.

This chapter on theatre lighting design is not going to make you a rigger or an electrician. It is important that young enthusiasts work under the supervision of a qualified and experienced adult and within compliance to the laws and health and safety best practice.

This chapter is also not going to give you one correct way to light your production. Let's rather think of this as an exploration of ideas or suggestions that you can try out. Some may be possible, others not. It will be largely dependent on your budget, the fixtures you have available, the technical time you have allocated to make your vision come to life... and most importantly, it will depend on the demands made by the script and/or director's vision.

Schedules exist for a reason! They keep everyone a little saner if you are all working towards the same goal and within the same time frame and they allow you to be realistic about what can be achieved in the time you have.

WHERE DO WE BEGIN?

Allow me to illuminate you!

It will come as no surprise to say that we begin with the script. What can we answer from a script? Details such as:

○ *Time of day – e.g. Is it morning or evening?*

○ *Location – e.g. Inside a house or in a leafy forest?*

○ *Mood – e.g. Is it dark and heavy? Or happy and light?*

The production concept is an important driving force in lighting design. What are you trying to highlight?

After reading the script, lighting designers must attend rehearsals and hold numerous meetings with the director to make sure that everyone is working towards the same goal. It's pointless having a warm and sunny lighting design when the director is trying to highlight the destruction of war. At this point it is helpful to understand...

THE AIMS OF LIGHTING DESIGN

Visibility: We need to see the actors and action. Sometimes, however, it's also about what we shouldn't see or can't see. By way of example: I once saw a beautiful production about a boy's obsession with darkness and his fear of light. In this production, darkness was as important as light.

To Reveal Shapes: This is particularly true of three-dimensional sets. Also in dance, where the aim is to highlight the body in space.

Support of the Genre and the Directorial Concept: Musical theatre is obviously different from realism and therefore the demands made on lighting are different. There are many different genres of theatre which include musical theatre, pantomime, ballet/dance, drama, realism and fantasy. Although there are no hard-and-fast rules, each one calls for a specific lighting style.

- *Musical Theatre: Often makes use of follow spots, saturated colours and dramatic shifts.*

- *Ballet/Dance: Often makes use of follow spots, side-lighting to reveal the human body in motion, and bright front-lighting (particularly in ballet).*

- *Drama: Often uses practical light fittings and general states.*

- *Realism: This is literally an attempt to create a 'slice of life', therefore colours tend to be realistic and in real time.*

- *Fantasy: Often uses non-realistic light sources (e.g. creative light sources such as torch or candlelight), shadow puppetry, and calls for dream-like states.*

Reinforcement: Lighting needs to reinforce the set and the costume designer's work. There is no point in putting a green light on an actress's red dress. It will make the dress look brown and the actress appear Martian.

Opus: What does the entire, composite picture look like?

Punctuation: Does the script, action or choreography call for a lighting change to highlight a specific moment? A director I work closely with refers to these moments as 'buttons', and together we use them to highlight a picture at the end of a song or dance.

Let the composite picture tell the story.

COLOUR ASSOCIATIONS

HOW DO WE USE COLOUR?

I'm often asked by new designers what colour to use. My standard answer is:

O *Refer back to the script. What time of day is it?*

O *What does the set design need?*

O *What will highlight the costume design?*

O *What is the genre of the production?*

Now, think of your own emotional response to colour. Moonlight coming in through a tower window onto a sleeping princess might be a pale blue or light gold. Whilst in a production of *Hamlet*, strong red back-light would draw attention to the loss of life and Hamlet's anger.

I suggest making your own list of colours and writing a list of associated emotions/ideas in the column next to it.

For example:

O *Red: Blood, anger, fire, drama.*

O *Dark Blue: Loss, alone, night.*

O *Light Blue: Clinical, white light, moonlight, sadness.*

O *Green: Envy, nature, evil.*

Now, make your own list and remember there are no right or wrong answers. Exploring colour in theatre is a never-ending journey. There are literally thousands of shades and hues to choose from. I find it useful to think of an artist creating and using a colour palette for a particular work.

It is important to understand the differences between warm and cold colours.

○ *Warm Colours: Red, amber, gold, yellow, pink, peach, orange.*

○ *Cold Colours: Blue, green, grey.*

○ *Neutral Colours: Lilac and lavender.*

Neutral colours complement both warm and cold colour spectrums.

I find it useful to make simple drawings of which area of the stage I want to light in a specific colour. Remember that lighting someone in strong, front, red light will not make their facial features clear. Perhaps this is what you looking for, but if not, consider using strong back light in a colour instead of front light.

LIGHTING POSITIONS

Lighting positions vary from one theatre to the next and depend largely on what type of space it is. A proscenium arch theatre is very different from a black-box studio. Understanding basic positions, however, is vital:

Front of House Lighting: Positioned in the auditorium which front lights the stage. Referred to as FOH. Predominantly used to light faces and create visibility.

Side Lighting: Positioned from the wings to side-light the action onstage. Widely used in dance, traditionally side-light fixtures are mounted on using either ballet stands, boom stands or ladders.

Cyc Lighting: Saturated colours used to light the back wall (the cyclorama).

Foot Lighting: Lighting positions along the front edge of the stage used to up-light the scenery and the actors. Often used in pantomime and melodrama.

Overhead Lighting: Positioned above the stage – or just in front of it – to provide top light and washes across the stage.

Back Lighting: Lighting positions behind and above the action used to create three-dimensionality and make actors look less 'flat.' I like to think of this position as my 'touched by an angel' or 'halo' lighting.

THE LIGHTING PLAN

This is the process of drawing a diagram showing the lighting choices you have made.

In professional theatre this drawing is to scale, and references important set design features. However, it can also be a simple drawing of your plan for the production. I cannot stress the importance of this drawing enough.

Not only does it serve as a record of your design for future productions, (or even if the production tours), it allows for later problem-solving and is particularly useful in focus sessions.

Divide the stage into sections – upstage, downstage, stage-right (opposite prompt), stage-left (prompt side), centre stage – and decide:

O *Which fixtures you are going to use to light which areas.*

O *Where you are going to hang your fixtures.*

O *What your colour choices are for each area in each scene.*

O *Whether you will use gobos.*

O *Where you will need specials.*

O *What colour washes you need.*

Draw it. Putting it all down on paper will help to clarify your ideas and provide practical solutions.

FOCUSING

Following the lighting plan, this is the process of pointing all generic lights in the right direction and at the right angle before 'locking' them off so that they don't swing loose. Here are the rules to remember:

- *Working at height is dangerous and must always be undertaken by a professional adult.*

- *Remember to keep the area around the ladder free of unnecessary crew.*

- *Everyone on ground level should wear hardhats, particularly if your lighting bars have to be rigged at their full height and can't be lowered to working height.*

- *Train everyone on stage to recognise the command of 'Heads!' and to take immediate action to move out the way because something overhead is being moved/dropped. This command is issued by the person up the ladder and for obvious reasons, all crew on the ground must not be making noise – they have to hear it being called!*

- *Make sure general washes are achieved for where you have planned them, and that your specials are the right size and shape.*

- *Ideally, focus sessions should be allocated in the production's get-in/bump-in schedule and adhered to. It is too dangerous for crew and actors to be working on the stage at the same time, as the working lights are switched off during this period.*

PLOTTING

There must be scheduled time allocated for:

- *The director and the lighting designer to agree on the lighting of each scene.*

- *The lighting programmer to punch or 'plot' the cues onto the lighting desk.*

116

○ *The stage manager to mark their script with the cue numbers and exactly when each cue should 'go'.*

○ *One of the crew (or more) to walk the stage so that you can see what the actors or dancers will look like in the different lighting states.*

Plotting onto a lighting desk enables the lighting designer to have a degree of control over each channel. The lighting desk controls the channel into which the fixtures are plugged or patched and is used to establish each cue's specific look.

During plotting, you want to select a fixture, a light you have placed, and select a level. This is usually a percentage. So let's say for the opening scene you want to fade in the blue FOH lights to 70% and at the same time bring up the magenta cyc lighting to 65%. There's your first cue.

There is no point in putting fifty fixtures on your plan if your budget only allows for ten, or if the theatre doesn't have sufficient power to run them all. Go back and revisit the aims of theatre lighting. Have you achieved visibility? Mood? Punctuation? How you plot these cues will depend on your lighting desk.

LIGHTING DESKS

Computerised lighting desks control channels in a number of ways:

○ *Faders/slides which can be pushed up/down to control intensity.*

○ *A numbered keypad where you can type in a value.*

○ *A wheel which can be dialled to control particular parameters such as intensity or, in the case of intelligent lights, colour and positions.*

All lighting desks have a grand master control fader which is used to adjust the output levels (intensity) of all the fixtures.

Submaster faders, by contrast, can be programmed to give you control over a specific group or groups of fixtures and to set their parameters.

Most lighting desks will allow you to record all your cues in numerical order and then play them back (make them live on stage) by pressing a GO button. Cues can be faded in and out by recording the fade time onto the desk. This means that when the GO button is pressed you get a smooth crossfade between one state and the next.

SMOKE MACHINES

Smoke machines are used for effects in theatre. They are useful in that they can aid both lighting and set design. In a production of *The Ladykillers*, I used a smoke machine from offstage to represent the passing steam trains.

Smoke machines are often used in dance productions and are advantageous when you want to create a smoke effect that clears relatively quickly. The disadvantages, however, are that they are often very noisy and require both power and DMX cables to run to them.

HAZE MACHINES

Haze in a theatre production is a thing of beauty. It makes the light beams visible and is far less noisy than a smoke machine. Also controlled via DMX, both machines can often be controlled directly from the lighting desk.

IN MY EXPERIENCE...

I once had to light the interiors of a number of small dolls' houses as if those inside had switched on the electricity. There was absolutely no way to run cables to each house as they were only on stage for a few minutes and the cast carried them on and off. To see them being plugged in would have ruined the magic of them lighting up. The houses could only hold small 12-volt batteries but I soon found that car indicator lights were small and could run from these batteries. The challenge was now to get them to 'switch' on without dimmer power – and all at the same time.

The issue was solved one morning as I opened my gate with a remote control device. I suddenly thought: 'How did that work? Could I use the same idea to solve my problem?' The answer was 'Yes.' Wiring the houses with a car indicator light bulb, a 12-volt battery and a remote receiver each, I could press the button on my remote and all the houses lit up magically without any visible wiring, and the theatricality of it was priceless!

In a production of *Sweeney Todd* for which I did the lighting design, there was a particular scene which called for a visual divide into three distinctly separate areas:

- *Mrs Lovett's pie shop downstage-right.*

- *Sweeney sitting centre-stage remembering his wife in a flashback which we could see above the pie shop.*

- *A ballroom scene downstage left.*

I lit the pie shop using realistic warm interior colours. The flashback scene above them I lit in rosy pinks representing the warm memory of his wife. Finally, I lit the ballroom scene in dark blues with footlight and cross-lights to make it look sinister, as this is the scene in which his wife is hurt. The result was a composite picture of Sweeney's memories all visible to the audience at the same time.

FINAL WORD

Hopefully your lighting design will be a great success. After the curtain falls, congratulate yourself. But, remember there's always room for improvement. Then, allow for reflection.

How could you have achieved that effect more successfully? Would you use the same colours again?

Challenge yourself. It's the only way to grow.

RESOURCES

TERMS

Blackout: Literally a black state. No visible lighting. All channels at 0%.

Crossfade: Quite literally a crossfade between one state and the next. This is achieved by programming an up time (the time it takes to lead into the next state) and a down time (the time it takes to fade the first state out) on the lighting desk.

Cue: Point at which the lighting changes.

Cyclorama: The back wall of a theatre stage, often lit with floodlights to create saturated even colour washes across the back of the stage.

Dimmer channel: Electrical fitting used to control intensity and crossfade of light output.

DMX: Standardised lighting signal protocol is DMX 512. It is used to carry commands from the lighting desk to the fixtures regarding intensity and crossfade times, and in the case of intelligent lights choices around colour, beam shape, gobo and intensity.

Follow spot: Fixture which is controlled by a human operator. It can move left and right, and pan up and down. It can also change colour by manually inserting a new gel into the tube of the fixture.

Fresnel: Type of lighting fixture. Identifiable by the concentric circles on its lens, with the ability to make the beam bigger and smaller only. Often used to achieve a wash of colour across stage.

G-Clamp: Clamp which secures lighting fixture to a lighting bar.

Gel: Coloured filter placed into generic lights to colour their light beams.

General: A number of lighting fixtures which combine to light the entire stage.

Gobo: Pattern plate inserted into profiles and some intelligent lights to reveal patterns (e.g. tree branches).

Intelligent lighting: Term given to fixtures which do not use dimmer channels but instead use DMX signal to control them. They receive signal from the lighting desk to a particular address entered into the fixture. This address ensures that the light receives information intended for only that light's operation. The address can be any number between 1 and 512 – the number of channels in a DMX universe. I like to think of DMX as a postman delivering a letter (information) to a particular address (fixture) telling it what to do and how to behave.

Intensity: How bright the light is. Measured on the lighting desk beween zero and one hundred per cent.

Iris: Inserted metal iris in a profile makes the light beam smaller. Like the iris in our eyes, it shifts (dilates or constricts) to control the amount of light that is coming out of the fixture.

Parcan: Type of lighting fixture, easily identifiable because it looks like a car headlight in a paint can. These lamps do not have separate lenses and reflectors and come in either narrow, medium or wide beams. No ability to shape the light output.

Patching: Process of plugging lighting circuits into dimmers. This is achieved by hard patching (physically manually plugging) and/or soft patching (on the lighting desk).

Playback: Term used to describe the 'playing back' of different lighting states during a show. At the most basic level, it is the process of setting the channels on the lighting desk to a specific intensity and then fading them up at the relevant cue so that the fixtures receive their particular commands.

Plotting: Process of programming states/cues onto the lighting desk.

Safety chain: Rated safety cable used between the lighting fixture and the batten to which it is attached to prevent lights falling in the event of clamp failure.

Special: Isolated area on stage usually achieved by a profile.

Splitter: Signal box which splits DMX signal from the lighting desk to various outputs.

Workers: Lights used to illuminate the stage and wings when stage lights are not in use.

Chapter Eight

PUBLICITY

Illa Thompson

A highly successful publicist, Illa Thompson owns
her own publicity company which she co-manages.
She also writes for a leading daily newspaper and is a
popular regular on radio.

'**M**eet Illa – she decorates lamp posts.' This was how I was once introduced by a friend and, of course, it is true! Hopefully, however, by the end of this chapter you will have a better understanding than my dear friend of all that is involved in publicising a production.

It is helpful to designate the publicity/marketing responsibilities of your production to a few specific people in the production team: ideally those with interest or experience in communications. Good admin skills, attention to detail and the ability to talk and write well are all beneficial.

For maximum efficiency, the publicity campaign should probably start three to four months prior to the show opening.

In this chapter we are going to consider the following:

O *What does publicity mean, exactly?*

O *Who is your audience?*

O *How can you reach them?*

O *What tools do you need?*

O *Who should be doing what?*

O *The basics of a PR campaign.*

O *The trusty General Press Release.*

PUBLICITY

What does it mean exactly?

Words like 'Marketing', 'Publicity', 'Advertising' and the term 'PR' are often all lumped together, and thrown about at meetings, but what do they actually mean?

Well, in a nutshell:

O *Marketing is selling to a consumer.*

O *Publicity is making something known to a consumer.*

O *Advertising is a paid-for space in the media.*

○ *Public Relations (PR) is the relationship between your product and the public.*

Now that we have a rough idea of what we are talking about, let's look at who we are talking to.

AUDIENCE

Who are they?

This may seem like an obvious question, but firstly you need to identify your target market and potential audience in order to find them and communicate directly and efficiently with them.

It may include:

○ *The families of the performers.*

○ *The friends of the performers.*

○ *The community/ies of the performers/families living in a particular area.*

○ *The neighbourhood or suburb where the production is being staged, or where cast/production members come from.*

The choice of production may help determine the language and demographics of the audience. For example:

○ *An Easter Passion Play could be targeted strongly towards a churchgoing audience.*

○ *A non-spoken-word production (mime, dance, etc.) could be marketed to a multilingual audience as well as the Deaf community.*

○ *A set text could be marketed towards those studying it.*

It is a helpful exercise for the publicity team to start the process by brainstorming around this question and identifying the production's ideal target audience in some detail before embarking on a campaign.

COMMUNICATION

How can you reach them?

Once you are familiar with your target audience, you need to look at how to reach them.

O *What do they listen to? Identify the radio stations.*

O *What do they read? Identify the newspapers/magazines/online platforms.*

O *What social media groups do they perhaps belong to?*

O *Where do they go? i.e. shops/restaurants/places of leisure/schools/ places of worship.*

TOOLS

What do you need?

Once you know where to look for the audience, the next step is identifying what tools you need to do so. Obviously depending on budget and capacity, an effective, far-reaching campaign would include the following:

Five Months (or more) Prior to Opening:

O *Encourage sold performances/block bookings/charity galas.*

O *Start compiling a database of supporters with email and SMS details.*

O *Magazine features.*

Four Months Prior to Opening:

O *Magazine diaries (notify those magazines which offer listing opportunities).*

O *Prepare your posters and flyers/pamphlets.*

Two Months Prior to Opening:

Write press release, take photos and have these ready for media.

- *Sell advertising space in production programme.*
- *Prepare opening-night invitations.*

One Month Prior to Opening:

- *Send opening-night invitations.*
- *Add your poster/artwork to social-media platforms, and prepare a campaign of posts.*
- *Send details of the production to your emailing list.*
- *Notify your SMS database of your production.*

RESPONSIBILITIES

Who should be doing what?

Before we jump into the campaign, we should make sure we have the right people and skills in the publicity team. Many schools, organisations and clubs have public relations and marketing people in their teams already, so the production publicity and marketing personnel should work together and support the existing marketing team.

SALES PERSON

Look for the person who:

- *Is well-connected.*
- *Has a large network of contacts.*
- *Has a persuasive manner.*
- *Has good phone etiquette.*

With the above skills, this go-getter can phone and email contacts to help secure block bookings and sold performances, as well as sell adverts in the programme.

PUBLICIST

Look for the person who:

○ *Writes well.*

○ *Has keen administration skills.*

○ *Is extremely organised.*

The publicist writes the media releases, organises interviews, oversees the design, print and distribution of invitations, posters, fliers and programmes. The publicist will also send out the gala invitations, collect the RSVPs, and do the ticket allocation and seating plan for the opening night.

DESIGNER/PHOTOGRAPHER

Who is the artistic one on the team? They will need to:

○ *Design the flyers, posters and programme.*

○ *Take photos for use in the press, posters, programmes and social media.*

Bear in mind that you may need to budget for professional printers to print the poster, fliers, programme and possibly tickets. You may even need poster elevation specialists who erect posters on designated poster sites such as lamp-posts and community notice boards.

SOCIAL-MEDIA SPECIALIST

Find the people in the team who have the most social-media savvy and task them to ensure a presence across platforms, and to post regular, interesting, concise updates. Make sure the content is as visual as possible, ideally a series of still photographs and short video clips. Encourage the entire cast and crew to share, like and comment. If there is money in the budget – it may be worth considering creating an online trailer, but make sure it looks professional.

THE CAMPAIGN

The basics of a PR campaign.

The campaign can be as far-reaching, creative and detailed as your time and capacity allows.

STEP ONE

Write a General Press Release (GPR). This is the most important and most utilised tool of the campaign. The GPR is used to motivate for block-bookings, to accompany photographs, to be submitted for listings, to motivate for interviews and features, and to appear as notices across the entire media spectrum.

STEP TWO

Familiarity. Get to know the company. Get useful biographical material from the performers and the production team. Find out where they live, studied and worked. Have they won any awards or accolades? What are their special interests and skills?

Anywhere you can create a link between your production and your target community, do so! For example, if the sound technician is also a local football player then a story can be targeted at the sports pages of the newspapers or on sports/football publications/websites, which would reach a whole new potential market.

STEP THREE

Photographs will set the tone of how the production is communicated and, together with the production's design and print media, plays a huge part in the visual branding of the production.

Get your photographer (or a good camera) and take publicity shots of the cast and company. Take shots of rehearsals, portrait shots, posed shots and action shots. Look online for inspiration. Make sure you have more than you will possibly need.

Personally, I rate good photographs highly. I am reluctant to start a campaign unless I have a selection of high-quality, professional publicity stills. The more varied and interesting, the better, and all captioned with the character and actors' names from left to right.
Even if budgets are tight, I will prioritise ensuring that I have good photographs They can make or break the effectiveness of a campaign.

STEP FOUR

Designing posters/flyers/banners. Do some research. Examine what works and what doesn't and why.

O *Rule of thumb: keep them simple and uncluttered.*

O *Remember they are a tool to create awareness about the show – not a work of art – so communicating the appropriate info is of paramount importance.*

O *Keep the copy simple: the company/producer's acknowledgement line; production name; venue; dates and ticketing details.*

Check local byelaws about what is and isn't permitted to be on posters displayed in the public domain.

STEP FIVE

Magazines are a hugely oversaturated market, so choose magazines carefully and think of a particular angle in each instance. If they offer a 'What's On' guide, send the GPR and a captioned photo to the designated person ahead of the deadline. If there is a well-known person in the cast of your production, or if there are any interesting or newsworthy personalities, suggest to the editor to consider them for a personality profile feature.

Try and send different photographs to a competing magazine to avoid similar photos appearing at the same time in rival publications.

THE GPR

The General Press Release.

Research: Know your production and the company.

Writing: The reader may only read the first paragraph so make sure it contains all the key information – i.e. the name of the production, an enticing description of it; and where and when it will be staged.

Your second, third and fourth paragraphs should provide further information:

O *Cast and production details.*

O *A more in-depth description of the production.*

O *Interesting features about the production.*

The final paragraph should be a summary of what has gone before, including booking/ticketing details and dates/times information.

Ideally, your GPR should be one page long, about 500 – 700 words.

It is protocol to conclude the release with the word 'ends', after which you can include a sentence along the lines of: 'Should you require more information or additional photographs, please contact the production publicist (name) on (email) and (phone).'

Once the press release is written, it should be sent out with captioned photographs to all available and appropriate media two months/six weeks ahead of opening.

Once the media are in possession of the GPR, it provides context for further suggestions and feature ideas.

FINAL WORD

Whilst your role in the production is to encourage ticket sales, remember that you are the public front of the show you present, so your energy and quality of communications are the prelude to what takes place on stage. Goodwill is the key word in publicity.

So be mindful of relationships, affirm supporters, and be gracious and diligent.

RESOURCES

TERMS

Ad campaign: A series of linked adverts with a single idea or theme.

Banner ad: A display advert that sits horizontally on a website or app, usually at the top or bottom of the page.

Blog: Short for 'web-log'. A regularly updated portion of a website containing informative posts. A vlog is a similar 'video-log'.

Call-to-action: A button, image or clickable link on an advert, email or website that directs a visitor to take action – e.g. 'Subscribe now', or 'Buy your tickets here.'

Content: Term used to describe the material used in online marketing.

Cross-channel targeting: Targeting users across different channels (Facebook, X, Instagram, YouTube, TikTok) with adverts.

Hashtag: A word or phrase preceded by the # symbol. Using recurring hashtags allows users to see all related posts. A major event will usually have an official hashtag.

Inbound link: Link from an external site that points to your website.

Lead: A person or company who has shown some interest in your product in some way.

Marketing strategy: The plan for creating awareness of your production. It must include the 4 Ps: Production, Price, Place and Promotion.

Meme: Any popular image or text (or both) that is shared and spread quickly.

Reach: The total number of people exposed to your advert over a specific period of time.

SEO: Search Engine Optimisation is the practice of trying to gain more traffic from internet searches by using keywords and link-building.

Target audience: The group of people identified as the intended recipients of marketing and advertising messages. Marketing can be adjusted to suit different target audiences.

Chapter Nine

PLANNING

Extra tips and worksheets to assist with planning
your production.

ESTABLISH GOALS

Before starting any journey, it's a good idea to know where you're going and why. You don't want to get halfway through your production process and have forgotten why you started in the first place. If your main goal is for everybody to have fun, the minute it stops being fun means you've lost sight of your goal. You might even intend for your production to achieve several goals at once. Write them down. Keep them realistic. Perhaps even list them in order of importance.

Here are some examples:

- *To have fun.*
- *To develop talent.*
- *To showcase talent.*
- *To attract students to study theatre.*
- *To provide an opportunity for the community to work together.*
- *To raise funds for a worthy cause.*
- *To establish unity in the club/school/community.*
- *To celebrate a milestone.*
- *To entertain.*

THE PRODUCTION

Choosing your production.

There is always the temptation to stick with a familiar genre, but consider all the possibilities. Understanding the different types of productions will help you to select an exciting and appropriate choice.

You may have to give up your lifelong dream of producing and directing a certain musical if you don't have the abilities in your cast to support it. Basically, the cast you have (or know you can find) should determine the type of production you choose.

Consider the talent you have. The production should stretch them but not frustrate them. Consider their age. Both the content and the physical demands of the production should be age-appropriate.

A BOOK MUSICAL

This is a musical play consisting of a well-constructed story including song and dance. Music, lyrics and script all work together to develop the characters within the story – e.g. *Annie*, *The Sound of Music*, *Fiddler on the Roof.*

There are also sung-through musicals where, in addition to the songs, most of the dialogue is sung – e.g. *Les Misérables, Evita.*

An operetta is a sung-through musical in a more classical style – e.g. anything by Gilbert and Sullivan.

A MUSICAL REVUE

A collection of songs along a similar theme, loosely linked with original dialogue or a storyline. Your theme can be based on the following:

○ *The music – e.g. an artist or a genre.*

○ *A theme relevant to your target audience – e.g. Teenage Tortures.*

○ *Both – e.g. one artist's music can be used as a backdrop for an important local story.*

A PLAY

Whether it's a drama or a farce, classic or contemporary, a play is an excellent way to develop dramatic or comedic skills. It is also a sensible route to take if you don't have great singers in the cast.

A VARIETY CONCERT

Everyone gets a moment to shine in a variety concert. It allows young performers to showcase their own particular talents. But if you are going to stage a variety concert, make sure there is *variety*. Avoid an endless evening of vocal solos.

A PUPPET SHOW

These can be loads of fun especially if each performer gets to 'adopt' a character. They make the puppets themselves, develop the character and give it a voice. This is especially great for facilitating teamwork.

A SOIRÉE

This can be a gathering of people for the purposes of musical performance. The secret of the soirée is to keep it short and sweet. Better to hold a soirée every Sunday evening for a month than try and pack fifty musical performances into one evening.

RANDOM IDEA GENERATOR

This random idea generator is a fun way to break out of old mindsets. Download the resources pack from www.nickhernbooks.co.uk/curtain-up and then print out the following tables, cut out each of the titles and place into three separate bags for Venue, Genre and Style.

Each member of your production team can choose one paper slip from each bag. You might laugh at the idea of doing a Caribbean Dance Drama on the back of a truck, but then... why not? This is also a great challenge for impromptu drama sessions and improvisation workshops. Have fun!

VENUE	
GYMNASIUM	PLAYGROUND
FOOTBALL FIELD	CHAPEL/CHURCH
SWIMMING POOL	LECTURE THEATRE
BENEATH A TREE	QUADRANGLE
LIBRARY	WAREHOUSE
STREET	TRUCK
PROMENADE	MIDDLE OF HALL
MARQUEE	PROMENADE
CLASSROOM	PUB

GENRE	STYLE
BOOK MUSICAL	OLD B&W MOVIES
MUSICAL REVUE	MELODRAMA
PLAY	KABUKI
FARCE	FANTASY
SHAKESPEARE	FUTURISTIC
VARIETY SHOW	ELIZABETHAN
CHILDREN'S PLAY	VICTORIAN
MIME	AFRICAN
DANCE DRAMA	CARIBBEAN
MURDER MYSTERY	EASTERN
PUPPET SHOW	BOLLYWOOD
MULTIMEDIA SHOW	GOTHIC
ROCK CONCERT	CARTOON
OPEN MIC	MEDIEVAL
PARODY	1920s
PANTOMIME	1930s
ROMANCE	WW1
POETRY PROGRAMME	USA 1950s
TWO x ONE-ACT PLAYS	UK 1960s
OPERETTA	1970s
CHORAL VERSE	1980s

THE PRODUCTION TEAM

When putting together a production team, choose people who are passionate about the project, are good at what they do and who have creative ideas. We often think we can do it all. But the best results are when we are open to input from others whose strengths are different to our own.

Understanding the role of each member of the production team will help you to choose wisely. Base your decisions on the needs of your particular production.

THE CORE PRODUCTION TEAM

Those working *on* the production.

Director: The centre of all things. This is the person responsible for the creative direction of the production. The entire cast, production team and crew answer to the director and attempt to bring their vision to life.

Musical Director: The MD is responsible for directing the band/ orchestra, or creating the backing tracks. Their duties may include musical arrangements.

Vocal Director: This may be the same person as the MD. The epitome of patience, the vocal director is responsible for teaching the cast all the songs, harmonies, diction and dynamics.

Répétiteur: The rehearsal accompanist. This could be your musical or vocal director if their sight-reading is fluent enough. Having a pianist at rehearsals allows for greater flexibility and, because you don't have to wait every time for that exact place in a backing track, more effective time management.

Choreographer: A good choreographer understands that dance within a musical production is about storytelling as well as interpretation of the music.

Company Manager: Usually a member of the cast, but does not have to be. Duties can entail meetings with the cast regarding their general well-being, vocal and physical warm-ups, and rehearsing areas that need tightening up.

Set and Costume Designer/s: The designer/s must be familiar with the venue, the production, the era, the budget and the director's vision. This may be one person or a whole team.

Lighting Designer: Works closely with the director, set designer, costume designer and stage manager to plan the lighting requirements for the production.

Sound Designer: Plans the sound requirements. Liaises with the musical director.

THE ADMIN TEAM

Those working *for* the production.

Producer: The person or organisation who is making the production possible. In the professional theatre, they are either putting up the money themselves, or have resources available to them. Although they rely on the director for creative control, they sometimes have a say over the content of the show. It is the producer who generally appoints the director.

Secretary: The oil in the machine. The production secretary is responsible for the budget and all the payments. They may also organise schedules, transport and correspondence.

Publicist: Compiles press releases and photos. Publicises the show using media within the budget – e.g. radio, newspapers, social media, flyers, posters.

Poster/Programme Designer: Graphic artist who works according to the production team's brief.

Theatre Manager: Controls all areas of the venue including licences and permissions.

FOH Manager: Front-of-house manager at the theatre/venue. Manages the ticket sales and the foyer/s on show nights.

THE CREW

Those working behind-the-scenes *during* the production.

Stage Manager: Has absolute authority over the stage area from get-in to the theatre till the production closes. All cast and crew answer to the stage manager.

ASM: Assistant stage manager/s. May also be backstage assistants to other designers and technicians.

Lighting Technician: Operates the lights for each performance.

Spotlight Operator: Operates manual spotlight where necessary.

Sound Engineer: Runs the sound for each performance.

Props Master: Manages all props backstage.

Stage Hands: Crew members moving the scenery and assisting backstage where needed.

Flyhands: Crew members operating the fly bars. Cued by the stage manager.

Of course, you could have people doubling up on some of these roles. Bear in mind, however, that the best combinations are roles that don't overlap on the timeline. For example, a member of the production team may choose to join the crew because their creative role ends as the technical role begins.

BUDGET

Your creative spirit will conjure up exciting possibilities that will dance before you with gleeful abandon only to be captured and strangled by our old enemy: the budget.

Finance will influence your choices more than any other element of your production, so begin as you intend to continue. As you shape your budget, bear the following costs in mind:

Rights: A book musical can mean a huge outlay of money before you've even sold a ticket, although a well-known musical can sell more tickets.

Venue: Even a venue can have a following. It's easier to get an audience to a lovely theatre than to an abandoned warehouse, especially if they are regular attendees at the theatre. Don't forget to include theatre rentals in your budget.

Set: The set design, materials and labour can involve considerable cost in musicals and plays.

Equipment: Staging, lighting and sound equipment can all be costly if not included in the venue costs.

Professionals: Some amateur dramatic societies or schools will bring in music and dance professionals to assist them on the production team. This is a great idea but they will need to be paid.

Costumes and props: Both materials and labour need to be included in your budget, and don't forget costume laundry after the production.

Transport: Some of your cast might need assistance with transport costs.

Programmes: Budget for design and printing. However, whether they are sponsored by local business and/or you sell them, the programmes should pay for themselves.

Posters: Design, printing and distribution, unless online only.

Rehearsal venue: If you do not have a free hall at your disposal, you could rehearse elsewhere, but the space (or marked area) must be the same size as the performance area in the venue.

Publicity: Ticket sales are necessary to offset some or even all of your costs, and in order to sell tickets you have to make people aware of the production.

Here is a sample budget spreadsheet, downloadable from
www.nickhernbooks.co.uk/curtain-up

NO	ITEM	BUDGET	ACTUAL COST
1	PRODUCTION RIGHTS		
2	MUSIC LICENCE FEES		
3	OTHER LICENCE FEES		
	LEGALS SUBTOTAL		
4	PERFORMANCE VENUE		
5	REHEARSAL VENUE		
6	SET-BUILDING VENUE		
7	OTHER VENUES		
	VENUES SUBTOTAL		
8	DIRECTOR		
9	MUSIC/VOCAL DIRECTOR		
10	CHOREOGRAPHER		
11	PRODUCTION SECRETARY		
12	STAGE MANAGER		
13	RÉPÉTITEUR		
14	OTHER		
	CREATIVE TEAM SUBTOTAL		
15	SET DESIGN		
16	SET MATERIALS		
17	SET-BUILDING LABOUR		
18	EXTRA STAGING		
19	OTHER		
	SET SUBTOTAL		
20	PROPS DESIGN		
21	PROPS MATERIALS		
22	PROP-BUILDING LABOUR		
23	OTHER		

	PROPS SUBTOTAL		
24	COSTUME DESIGN		
25	COSTUME FABRICS		
26	COSTUME LABOUR		
27	COSTUME HIRE		
28	OTHER		
	COSTUMES SUBTOTAL		
29	LIGHTING DESIGN		
30	LIGHTING EQUIPMENT		
31	LIGHTING CREW		
32	OTHER		
	LIGHTING SUBTOTAL		
33	SOUND DESIGN		
34	SOUND EQUIPMENT		
35	SOUND CREW		
36	OTHER		
	SOUND SUBTOTAL		
37	SCRIPT PRINTING COSTS		
38	SHEET MUSIC		
39	BACKING TRACKS		
40	OTHER		
	SUPPLIES SUBTOTAL		
41	POSTER DESIGN		
42	POSTER PRINTING		
43	DISTRIBUTION		
44	PUBLICITY COSTS		
45	OTHER		
	PUBLICITY SUBTOTAL		
46	PROGRAMME DESIGN		
47	PROGRAMME PRINTING		
48	OTHER		

	PROGRAMME SUBTOTAL		
49	MAKE-UP ARTIST/S		
50	MAKE-UP SUPPLIES		
51	OTHER		
	MAKE-UP SUBTOTAL		
52	TRANSPORT		
53	OTHER		
54	OTHER		
55	OTHER		
	EXTRAS SUBTOTAL		
	GRAND TOTAL		

BUDGET-SAVING IDEAS

Family: Find out if any of the cast's family members have talents you can utilise – e.g. costume design and making, programme design, set design and construction, prop-making, sound and lighting.

Retirement homes: You'd be surprised how many elderly people would jump at the chance of being involved in a theatre project. Make up a list of requirements and tap into their years of experience and knowledge.

Choreographer: If you do not have a choreographer, consider asking the local dance-school teachers if they will each choreograph one number (or two, depending on how many dance studios there are) as their contribution to the school/charity/community. In return, you could advertise their dance schools in the programme.

Vocal direction: If any of your cast members have private singing teachers, give them an extra copy of their sheet music and ask them to work on their songs in their lessons.

Publicity: If you are a school or charitable organisation or donating the profits from your ticket sales, you could get free publicity. Community members raising money for charity is a good story. Start social-media pages for your production and get the cast to invite all their friends to join.

Sponsors: Ask local businesses to sponsor some of your expenses. It can be good publicity for them, but sometimes they just like to be involved in the community. Donations are useful but businesses generally prefer to have an area of responsibility – e.g. costumes sponsored by GetFit Gym; programmes sponsored by PrintHouse.

Rehearsal venue: If a church or school is willing to contribute to your project, a church hall or a school drama centre is a good rehearsal space, but make sure they won't mind you marking out your performance area on the floor with masking tape.

Cheap costuming: Charity shops are great for sourcing costumes. Small fabric flaws usually can't be seen on the stage so buying budget fabric at waste centres is also a good option.

Recycling centres: You can often source a lot of set-building/puppets/props materials from recycled waste. All you need is a van and some time.

Simplicity: Keep set design simple. If your lighting design is good you may even be able to do without scenery. The same applies to costumes. The simpler, the cheaper.

Crew: Students who are studying drama at university might be interested in working as crew on your production for the work experience.

FINAL WORD

To be prepared does not mean that there is no space for creativity. On the contrary, preparation removes unnecessary distractions, leaving your mind free to create.

Planning keeps you ahead of the game and makes it possible for your rehearsals to be exactly what they are intended to be. So plan – and then play!

NOTES

NOTES

NOTES